TOMORROW IS TOO LATE

TOMORROW
IS TOO LATE

An Autobiography

RAY MOORE

edited by
TREVOR BARNES

Constable · London

First published in Great Britain 1988
by Constable and Company Ltd
10 Orange Street, London WC2H 7EG
Copyright © 1988 Ray Moore
Reprinted 1988 (six times)
All rights reserved
Set in Linotron Ehrhardt 12pt by
Rowland Phototypesetting Ltd
Bury St Edmunds, Suffolk
Printed in Great Britain by
St Edmundsbury Press Ltd
Bury St Edmunds, Suffolk

British Library CIP data
Moore, Ray
Tomorrow is too late
1. Great Britain. Radio programmes.
Broadcasting – Biographies
I. Title   II. Barnes, Trevor, 1951–
791.44'092'4

ISBN 0 09 468700 5

TO ALMA

who has held my hand through the brightest of days
and the darkest of nights, and who has given me
the happiest moments of my life

INTRODUCTION

There are so many people to thank for their help in producing this slim volume, that it may seem invidious to single out one or two for special mention. But both Alma and I owe a profound debt of gratitude to Joan and Maurice Potter, two very dear friends whose love and kindness pulled us through some very dark days, and in whose idyllic cottage, lost deep in the Sussex countryside, most of the book was written.

I must mention also Julie Pearce who managed to make sense of my spidery longhand scrawl and amazingly produced a comprehensible typescript.

And the publisher, Robin Baird-Smith, who endured the tantrums of a 'first time writer' with great fortitude and understanding.

Lastly, my sincere thanks must go to the multitude of listeners, colleagues and friends who have given me so much laughter over the years, and whose support in recent months has been invaluable.

In spite of what has happened, I have been so lucky in having forty-six wonderful years, doing a job I adored with people I loved. I naturally would have liked it all to go on a little longer, but as Alma often used to say 'You never know when you've had enough' – Moore by name and more by blooming nature!

For all we know, we may never meet again,
We come and go like ripples in a stream,
We won't say goodbye until the very last minute

[1]

My earliest memory is of VE Day. May 1945, Cherry Close, Liverpool. I was a weedy kid, three years old, ill as usual and totally unaware that somewhere up there a plan was being hatched for me that afternoon. It was to be every bit as decisive as the blinding flash on the road to Damascus, but as the nearest road to us led to Bootle no-one should be surprised that the revelation took a rather less dramatic form. It was a turning point all the same.

One of my mysterious stomach aches (which seemed to plague my sickly childhood years) had hit me again, laying me low enough to feel justified in refusing my dinner but not sufficiently so, I secretly hoped, for me to miss out on the street party which our neighbours had organised. I was used to my mother's bizarre remedies on occasions like this – heady cocktails of liquid paraffin known as 'opening' medicine, a mixture of bread and milk which we called 'Pobs', or a spoonful of plum jam containing half an aspirin – and I knew all of them were useless. So, I think, did my mother who decided accordingly that what medication might fail to cure, indignation would. 'If you can't eat cabbage you can't eat jelly so you'll have to stay inside.' And so to the blinding flash.

I now see that little front room of ours with a vivid clarity. I sat there sullenly looking out on a sunny afternoon as all the other kids and their mums tucked into cakes and buns and bottles of pop, their shouts and laughter deepening the silence of the darkened room where I was now unwillingly marooned.

Mum switched on the big old bakelite wireless and exotic names like Kalundborg, Hilversum, Alsace and Nantes suddenly lit up. A man called Alvar Liddell began to read the news and in that very instant a strange magic worked its unforgettable spell. As I listened to that lovely voice the hubbub outside faded into a distant echo. I listened and listened knowing from the deepest part of my tiny soul that my life would be radio. That was what I wanted to do. That was what I had to do. As that warm reassuring voice filled the room everything else ceased to matter and it was as if my vocation and my destiny were suddenly being made clear to me. From then on radio would be my reason for living. It was an overwhelming experience, a religious moment which lives with me still.

But if my career in broadcasting began with an exhilarating swiftness then with a cruel irony, twenty five years later, it ended with equally unexpected speed when cancer was diagnosed. This glorious thing, radio to which I had been wedded for so long was, in an instant, snatched from me forever.

The news of the cancer seemed to unlock a door for many thousands of people. For a time it was as if I was getting more reaction from listeners for contracting a terminal disease than for anything I had ever done as a broadcaster. As one of my friends said, 'It's one hell of a way to get yourself on to the front pages'. People sent me letters by the sackful, often written in green ink extolling some of the most bizarre cures imaginable. I can now compile a list of every faith healer and spiritualist in Great Britain, not to mention the rest of the world. From Bolivia to Taiwan, from Nepal to Southern Australia, I have addresses of obscure cancer clinics and mysterious specialists. Quite where one is supposed to find the money to get to these curious outposts is never made clear. I do not want to end up dead *and* bankrupt.

Many of the letters contained elements of the purest black comedy. One lady informed me that her fifteen year old fox terrier had exactly the same sort of cancer as mine. Another took the trouble to write in to say her husband died 'of what you've got'. And the cures they suggested. 'Live on beetroot juice for three months', 'my granny cured her cancer by eating only carrots and grape juice' . . . with dietary obsessions such as these to contend with I now see why I had so many 'regular' listeners. And for some reason, quite beyond me, many of the cures involved the removal of all my teeth so that not only would I have had a stomach racked with a surfeit of beetroot and carrot, I would also have ended up resembling Old Mother Riley or Gabby Hayes. Perhaps it was all just to provide a little comic relief so that the cancer would seem a trivial side issue.

On one occasion, one of my neighbours turned up on the doorstep one day and listened, with what seemed to me undue relish, to the full story of my disease. I told him that a combination of radiotherapy and radical surgery had been suggested as possible solutions, that huge doses of radiation would be followed by an operation to remove my teeth, three quarters of my jaw and half of my tongue and that the resulting facial damage would be shorn up with bits of bone taken from my foot. I told him how the doctors had spelt out the options and gone into the most elaborate details surrounding the intricacies of their particular art.

At the end of all this my friend looked impressed. 'Gosh', he said, as if we were talking about forthcoming plans to build an extension to the kitchen, 'that must have been a very interesting experience for you'. Being told you have two years left to live but that it could extend to two and a half or maybe three years if you consent to radiation sickness and the full scale demolition of your face generates many emotions but I have to say that 'interest' is not one of them.

On balance, though, most people expressed a genuine sense of shock and sorrow at the news and were anxious to help me in any way they could. I had offers of holidays in boarding houses in Mousehole and free coach trips to Lourdes. Incidentally, I received a number of Lourdes cigarette lighters. I had never realised before that Our Lady was a smoker . . . fond of Churchman's No. 1's, no doubt. Coming from Liverpool I was automatically assumed to be Roman Catholic and, as a result, bottles of Lourdes water would turn up by the crateful along with, in one consignment, a scrap of old, rough cloth. It looked like a one hundred year old piece of Elastoplast, but was supposed to be a relic of St Phoebe's knickers or something and imbued with remarkable properties. Application to the affected part for a period of six months would, I was told, do the trick.

Looking back on all this, if I had known I was so popular on the radio, I would have demanded more money from the BBC.

My great dilemma is how to live an ordinary life now that an extraordinary event like cancer has become part of it. I refuse to see myself as a cancer 'victim', as a problem on legs and I do not want to make a career out of being a patient. Terry Wogan has been a good friend to me over the years. He is a warm man whom I admire very much but when I got offers of appearing on his show I had to turn them down for just these reasons. I am Ray Moore first, and a cancer sufferer second, and I do not want to be fodder for another newspaper story or TV programme on 'courageous old Ray'. For one thing I am not at all courageous and I have wept buckets over all this but, more important than that, I simply want to get on with living a full life which is not conditioned and regulated, dictated and restricted by disease. Of all the reactions I have had so far I cherish most that of an old lady I met the other day in the village. She came up to me and without a trace of self-consciousness said, 'I read about you the other day in the newspaper. I say, isn't it all a dratted nuisance?'

Now that is the sort of approach I like. That wonderfully low key, English way of putting it. 'What a dratted nuisance', she said, and then changed the subject to the weather. I appreciated that.

So why, if I am claiming to play down my condition, am I writing all this? The first reason, I suppose, is that while I am not a regular church goer, I am by temperament religious and committing emotions and recollections to print is, I suppose, in the nature of a confession. The second, and far more compelling motive, is to put my wonderful years in radio and TV into some kind of perspective. In my darker moments I have wondered what the point of all this has been. To be given personal happiness and professional fulfilment only to have them snatched from me as randomly as they were bestowed. But then I stop the moaning, fling open the shutters of my soul and allow the sunshine to come streaming in. I have nothing to feel sorry about. When I go to the hospital and see some of the youngsters in the wards, bald and ashen faced, then I am filled with sadness and I cannot begin to understand why someone so young should be made to suffer. It is then that I start screaming at God for an explanation. But me? What do I have to complain about? I am forty six, I have had twenty five fantastic years of fun and laughter in the business and now I am being told to ease up a little. That's all. So I write this as a way of counting my blessings. Sure, it is the obituary of Ray Moore's career, but Ray Moore the man is still very much around.

And in this business it is wise not to have too grand an idea, anyway, of what your career really amounts to. I am often haunted by the account I shall have to give of myself at the Pearly Gates. 'I have given you a good voice, Moore', He will say, 'and a certain facility with words. And what have you done with these gifts and your life?' I will shuffle uneasily from foot to foot and be forced to tell the truth, 'Well, I was the guy who made the funny comments between the records on the early show'. Will He be impressed, I wonder? He certainly could not be less overawed by my achievements than a cab driver recently. I climbed into his taxi and exchanged a few words with him when suddenly he said, 'Guv, I know your voice. Where do I know your voice from?' I let him go on a bit without putting him out of his misery and told him I hadn't been in his cab before so I didn't know how he knew me. 'It's driving me nuts', he said, 'I dunno your face but I know your voice.' Eventually we arrived at our destination and as I was paying him the fare, the penny dropped. 'I've got it,' he shouted with triumphant satisfaction, 'I know who you are. You're the Speaking Clock!'

In my time I have attracted a sizeable proportion of listeners who seem to have had only a tenuous connection with reality. All the poor souls who reckoned that if I spoke louder they would overcome the problems of a flat battery or those who complained if I had a cold or 'flu. 'Disgraceful', wrote one lady, 'infecting the nation like that. Now we'll all get it!' And one favourite of mine. Benjamin Brittain Forshaw, who used to write in gloriously huffy letters. 'Moore! Heard your appalling shambles on the wireless this morning. Another two hours of unutterable drivel and cliché-ridden claptrap. Nothing but infantile humour totally lacking in wit. Sincerely, Benjamin Brittain Forshaw. P.S. Insulting letter follows.'

And there was another character who struck up a similarly endearing love/hate relationship. One Garry Jackson, who has, you might say, a position of 'grave' responsibility at a place called the Cranley Crematorium in Coventry. He would write very entertaining funereal letters edged in black saying how he was the head grave digger and had hundreds of people under him. One morning when I sounded particularly rough he sent me a claim form. He reckoned he had spotted me first so the crematorium had first refusal. In fact most people said they only really tuned in to me because I sounded as rough as they felt first thing in the morning and quite a few women said they could not tolerate me at any price, but used to listen to me because they were already up doing their washing on the cheap rate.

Radio is a very personal medium and people have definite likes and dislikes. The voice – especially a disembodied voice coming from a transistor radio on the sideboard – is a very curious thing. Lots of folk think that on radio I sound as if I have a moustache. I have never quite understood what special quality a moustache adds to the *vox humana* but clearly my audience does. An appearance on TV is guaranteed to provoke a rush of letters of complaint from people who insist that the voice they heard the night before was coming out of the wrong face. I am happiest when I am heard but not seen, a reaction which may have something to do with a leaked memo from a BBC executive which I caught sight of many years ago. The relevant BBC authorities, it said, had severe reservations about my appearing on television, reservations mainly arising out of my face! Not that it worried me at all. I am really a radio man anyway.

For one thing the radio is so intimate and capable of establishing a direct personal relationship between me and the listener. It is mightily influential, too, and I had to be careful what I said since people had a tendency to believe every word they heard. I would have a whole sequence of silly phrases to introduce or follow a record and used them quite liberally in a flippant sort of way. After a particular record I liked I might have said, 'That was the best record ever made since Rudyard Kipling baked his first exceedingly good cake' and I would have thought no more about it. One morning, however, we had an angry phone call from a man running a National Trust house in Kent which had been the home of the great writer. Evidently coach parties had been turning up at the gates asking to see the actual kitchen where Rudyard Kipling had baked his first exceedingly good cake!

That was not the only embarrassing corner I painted myself into. One really quite unforgivable incident surrounded an apparently harmless record request by a lady for her old mum who was about to celebrate her ninety eighth birthday and who was in rather critical health. The record chosen was a favourite of hers, 'My Way' by Frank Sinatra. Both my producer and I saw nothing inappropriate about this until it was actually on the turntable going out on air. The opening line, you may remember, goes, 'And now the end is near and so I face the final curtain.' In circumstances like that a discreet silence is the only possible reaction followed by a speedy move on to the next record.

There was a very special feel to my early morning show. It had a surreal quality about it which owed much to that shadowy, vulnerable time of the day when half the world is beginning to rub its eyes for the hours ahead and the other half is fast asleep. I felt a sort of complicity with my listeners as though we, the early risers, had the privilege of sharing a strange and unique insight into the ways of the world, denied those who lived the nine to five life.

'You lose track of the days working on nights, don't you, Ray?' With these profound words my driver, the wonderfully lugubrious Sid Sutton, would greet me at four thirty in the morning and transport me in the BBC hearse down the Old Kent Road like Lord Muck just as the city was coming to life. Chaps in dinner jackets who had just been poured out of night clubs rubbed shoulders for a moment with technicolour punks lounging round Trafalgar Square. One of my favourites was a young punk girl with long black hair which she had glued vertically on top of her head. It stood about two feet high and gave you the impression she was wearing a stove pipe hat. Then there was the outlandish character who wore a full white wedding gown complete with a posy of flowers, black hobnail boots, and a thick black moustache. All this was rich material from which to cobble together a couple of hours of the controlled anarchy that passed for my radio show.

At that time of the morning you were aware of two separate worlds which existed side by side but which never came into contact with each other. The daytime world and the night-time world which supported independent, self-contained lives. Strange little vans pottered down the Old Kent Road representing firms which simply did not exist in the daylight. Two or three times a week I used to see one bearing the puzzling legend, 'The Ferret Cleaning Company'. It set me asking rather searching questions. I mean if you had a ferret why would you let it get dirty in the first place? And why should you pay money to have it cleaned afterwards anyway? 'Hat Maintenance' was another bewildering sign I regularly saw. Is there a market for that sort of thing? Do people really go to the milliner's, hand over a trilby and ask for it to be put through its routine service as part of some sartorial MOT? When I saw juggernauts going up the hill with 'Brain Haulage' on the side I often thought that this was carrying transplant surgery rather too far. And, most baffling of all, an establishment called, 'The Annual Lamp Company'. Picture a line of Hogarthian grotesques hanging around a gloomy factory somewhere for 364 days of the year waiting for the big moment – the annual switch-on. Funnily enough some weeks after I had mentioned this on the air I got a telegram from the company in question. Thank you for the mention, it said, and added at the bottom, 'PS Tonight's the night!'

The techniques you need to use on a television show are often quite different from the ones I relied on for my radio programme and I have to declare that from time to time I was deemed by some members of the viewing public to be not quite up to the job. I was the voice, for instance, on the last series of 'Come Dancing' hosted by Terry Wogan. Not being terribly 'au fait' with the world of haberdashery I omitted to mention how many silver sequins Mabel Quartbottom's mother had sewn on to her dress the night before. I should have realised the awful omission and been well prepared for the torrent of abusive mail which followed. 'Ray Moore's not describing the dresses properly', they wrote in their angry thousands. My reaction was to fire off letters in reply explaining that the mistake was entirely mine. That I had been foolishly labouring under the delusion that 'Come Dancing' was a *television* programme and that they could therefore see the dresses themselves. Ah, but that was not the point and no-one was mollified by my excuse.

A far more traumatic event much later threatened to bring my involvement with the world of Terpsichorean glitter to a premature end. It happened when I was working on a dance programme for Channel 4. The Tower Ballroom in Blackpool was very nearly the scene of my undoing – in both senses of the word. Bobbie Irvine, a professional dancer herself and an absolute stunner, was sharing the commentary with me on the night of a much publicised dancing competition. As a grand finale to this sparkling event, when all the results had been declared, Bobbie and I were supposed to sprint down the stairs from the gallery to be the first couple on the floor. This I judged to be unwise at the best of times, given that I have never learnt to dance and have trouble even walking these days. But I agreed. On the sweep down the stairs, to take the floor with Bobbie, my dinner suit, which had reached the end of its natural life, split into two separate legs from navel to back. We reached the floor, the band struck up, the spotlight fell on us and as the television cameras beamed this unforgettable image into three million homes I did a quick circuit of the Tower Ballroom with a clenched smile and buttocks clenched even tighter round the edge of two cylinders of trouser which slowly and inexorably slid down to my knees.

For many years I was the disembodied voice on the Miss World Competition. We used to rehearse the show until the crew were blue in the face and browned off in the bargain with my constant repetition of vital statistics and national costumes. Looking back on it all I now seriously wonder if some of the girls in the competition were not clinically sub-normal. Many of them seemed to take three days to learn how to walk in a straight line, although I have to concede that if you have never set foot outside the Hindu Kush then Kensington Gore on a wet November night would seem something of a culture shock.

By way of livening up this deadening routine I had the habit, at the final dress rehearsal before transmission, of writing a cod script to entertain the engineers on closed circuit. So, as the girls paraded before me, I would be whispering into the mike, 'Yes, this is Miss Alabama, personification of the lumpen proletariat and looking like a sack of potatoes popped up on tree stumps . . . And now Miss Guatemala who describes herself as 22 but who looks more like she's going on 50 to me, dressed as an exhibit in an Oxfam shop window.' My downfall on this particular occasion was that all this tasteless rubbish, instead of being relayed to the engineers only on closed circuit, was in fact being broadcast to everyone – competitors, relatives, management and hangers-on – over the Royal Albert Hall public address system. I was half throttled that night by, if I remember correctly, Miss Nigeria and Miss Sweden, while Miss Paraguay really put the boot in. Eric Morley, who announces the results in reverse order, was seen taking gulps of air from an oxygen cylinder and instructing his solicitors, while I was seen going several shades of red and planning a new career.

Somehow I survived the humiliation, and had the good fortune to work with Andy Williams the following year when he was selected to host 'Miss World'. He is a charming man with a dry wit and a complete absence of showbiz pretension. I spent a lot of time with him in rehearsal discussing his music and learning what I could from the great man. A couple of things stand out quite clearly about my encounter with him. The first was a remarkable physical transformation that came over him between rehearsal and performance, and the second was his 'spontaneous' delivery.

I noticed the physical change shortly before we were due to go live on air. During rehearsal Andy, a man of somewhat short stature, had been roughly on a level with me. Now, just a few hours later, he towered over me like a pantomime giant. I was at a loss to explain this astonishing transformation until I caught a glimpse of his shoes. They represented the most amazing feat (or should I say 'feet') of civil engineering I had been privileged to witness in my entire life. The shoes were constructed on a sort of cantilever principle which when viewed at close quarters gave the impression that Mr Williams was staggering about on half concealed stilts. Despite the lifts he gave an astonishingly polished performance, all the more impressive, I thought, for his ability to overcome another potentially damaging fault. Off the cuff remarks were not his strong point; indeed he had a chronic inability to remember anything. As a result, the whole evening hosted by Andy Williams in the vastness of the Albert Hall was conducted with the aid of what are known in the business as idiot boards – twelve feet square cards with the appropriate words held up in front of him. Every introduction and every link was scripted in advance and placed out of camera shot a few feet away from him. I remember the first card. It read 'Good evening. My name is Andy Williams'.

People in glasshouses, however, should not be tempted to chuck bricks. Especially if, like me, they are inclined to drop them from time to time. Whatever else Mr Williams' performance was, it was relaxed and confident and in complete contrast to the one occasion when I was reluctantly drafted in to fill a last minute gap.

If I am ever nervous – and in a long career nerves have not been unknown – my hands tend to shake. My voice would stay straight, calm and measured, but at the slightest sign of nerves the hands would get shaky. This presents no problem at all if you are out of vision but is a real handicap if you are suddenly in the spotlight, as I was, quite unexpectedly, on the night of the big event. It so happened that the principal presenter booked to host 'Miss World' that year decided to change his mind at the last minute and I, who was supposed to be providing only the voice over, was hastily recruited.

'There's nothing for it, Ray,' the director told me starkly. 'Transmission is in just over an hour and we can't get anybody else to stand in. You'll have to go on and do it.' I could feel the panic rising within me. As a radio presenter you may have millions of listeners but you only have an audience of one – the person who is doing the washing on the cheap rate and listening to you in the solitude of her own kitchen. 'Miss World', with three thousand people staring expectantly from the stalls and balconies of the Albert Hall and another 25 million sitting in homes or bars or factories waiting for a slick performance, is quite another matter. But what else could I do but take the stage?

For an instant I contemplated suicide but I think I would not have had time even for that. I was given a long silver hand microphone and shunted on stage for the big moment. As usual the voice remained ever so calm and controlled but my hands got an attack of the shakes. All the time I was introducing the show I was aware that my hands were wobbling about furiously. The following morning I read the reviews only to see Nancy Banks-Smith's highly appropriate comment. 'Ray Moore', she wrote with a keen eye for detailed absurdity, 'appeared holding a dying mackerel!'

If anything, I would say the nerves get worse as you get older. People often ask if I get nervous and it surprises them to hear that I do. As you gain experience you know just what can go wrong, you are aware of all the dangers surrounding any live broadcast and you realise, with a sort of professional chill, how far you could fall. When I was young I was never troubled by nerves. In the recklessness of youth, just a couple of years out of Liverpool, I felt I could do nothing wrong. They could throw anything at me and I would deal with it. Little did I suspect, as I was working my way up the radio ladder, that one day this rather cocky young lad from Cherry Close would be talking to 27 million people, as happened one year for the 'Miss World' Competition.

I should point out for the record that this particular evening was not destined to go down in the archives as one of the memorable broadcasting moments. It was memorable, in fact, only as a non event. On the evening of the show the engineers had decided to call a strike within an hour and a half of the transmission. Again the director summoned the great Ray Moore. 'You'll have to shoot off to Television Centre (where the strike wasn't on)', he told me, 'and simply go on at 9.25 to explain that as a result of industrial action we cannot unfortunately go ahead with Miss World tonight. Make it up as you go along.' I duly made my announcement and when the audience figures came in the following week my apology for there *not* being a Miss World topped the 27 million mark. The previous year the Miss World Competition itself had managed only 25 million!

I look back on those wonderful moments and, in the words of the cliché, they seem like only yesterday and, if I am honest, I have to say I am still starstruck by it all, still in love with the glamour of this business, even if it does seem to be over before I fully realised it was there. I often try to imagine what the sickly kid from Liverpool would have made of it if he had known what was in store for him when he grew up. I suspect that he would not have dared to believe it, that he would have huddled close to the bakelite wireless in the front room of No.2, Cherry Close and hardly dared hope that something so precious would eventually be within his grasp. But I am glad he worked at it, that part of him never lost sight of the vision and that he transformed his daydream into reality. How much I have changed since then; but even now, even after all this time, the little boy with the big ideas is still somewhere deep inside me.

[2]

By every natural law we should have been an ordinary suburban family. But we were definitely not. We were odd. We were different from the other families in the close in a way which struck me vividly at the time but which, for a young lad who had known nothing else, was next to impossible to define. Was it not strange, for example, to see my father arrive home at the wheel of a black hearse dressed in a black overcoat and black Homburg? Well, no, not really, when you think about it, because he was, after all, an undertaker. Even so, nobody else's dad drove a hearse and parked it outside the front door. For some reason we just stood out – never doing the things or living life the way everybody else did.

I was brought up in a cosy little urban cottage in Cherry Close off Cherry Lane in Liverpool. A cottage in Cherry Close. How romantic it sounds. The reality was rather different. A cottage meant a small semi detached house, two up, two down, with the pavement at the front and a small garden at the back. Cherry Lane evokes misleading connotations, too; a picture-book address which fails to conjure up the railway embankment looming up beyond our front doorstep, the cratered bomb site at the back and the evil smelling picture house on the corner. This cinema seemed to me, as an impressionable child, to reek of dark, evil goings on. The air surrounding it was heavy with the powerful pong of disinfectant and stale cigarette smoke and if ever there existed a place of infinite intrigue and debauchery this was surely it.

Home was the safe haven away from this sinister, shuttered temple to nightly pursuits. But home, though warm and welcoming, was odd enough. In small ways it struck me as a bizarre set-up, inhabited by parents who, in temperament and outlook, in personality and background, could not have been more different. My strongest recollection of my father is of him not being there. He was a mercurial sort of character, a bohemian at heart, unpredictable in his many enthusiasms, fascinating and infuriating by turns, lovable, loving and childlike. And very fond of the drink.

When he wore his black hat and overcoat he cut a dashing figure but his Edward G. Robinson build, with his thick black hair and sharp blue eyes made him a slightly threatening figure at times, too. In some ways I was rather frightened of him. For a long and crucial period in my childhood he was a shadowy figure in the background, alluded to by Mum and Gran (not always in the most complimentary of ways) and strangely absent from our lives.

When he did appear he often seemed like Father Christmas to me. Sometimes, he would turn up slightly mellow, laden with armfuls of Dinky toys for me, and other presents for my brother and sister who, at the time, were rather too young to appreciate what was happening. He had a puzzling dual personality which I, as a child found threatening one minute and exhilarating the next but which often sent Mum into a fury. I could not understand why he was not like the other kids' fathers and why it was that, even in his absence, his personality hung over this odd household I loved and called home.

A small detail comes to mind. I remember going to a friend's house and being baffled when I saw they had carpet in the bathroom while we had only lino. A moment's thought revealed the reason. When Dad had a wash standing by the basin he would strip to the waist and splash water by the gallon over his

[25]

neck and face as if it were some kind of cold douche. The bathroom sounded like and resembled Niagara Falls as torrents of soapy water cascaded carelessly to the floor. Pretty soon the room bore all the marks of a minor natural disaster – and that was why we had lino. But this, as I say, is a tiny detail. Before revealing more of this marvellous man I should first sketch in a little of his own origin.

My Dad was a stocky, barrel-chested man who looked like a bulldog on its hind legs. A Liverpudlian to his boots he harboured a life long delusion that he was really Manx because the Isle of Man had been his family home for generations. Indeed to my Dad his swarthy features and blue eyes were proof positive that he was descended from a line of gallant sailors shipwrecked with part of the Spanish Armada off the southern coast of the island. The fact that this was a romantic cock and bull yarn did not worry him a bit, after all was not the final, conclusive proof that his surname was Moore? The connection was obvious to him alone and confirmed that he was the latest in a swashbuckling line of Spanish or 'Moorish' ancestors!

His pedigree was a most confusing affair altogether – toing and froing between Liverpool and the Isle of Man. He was one of a pair of identical twins of whom neither had much recollection of their natural parents. He was born in Liverpool in 1907. When he was two his mother died and he was packed off to the Isle of Man to be reared by an elderly aunt for a couple of years. He returned to Liverpool, then aged four, when his own father remarried. But he was to face premature bereavement again when his father was killed in the Great War leaving young Bill and his twin brother, George, to be brought up by their stepmother. Shortly after their father's death the two of them went back to the Isle of Man with their stepmother.

She was, by all accounts, a rather harsh woman and as a result Dad had a hard life. He was never allowed to celebrate birthdays, never had parties and was not permitted to have anything like a conventional childhood. His stepmother seemed to make no allowance for the two brothers letting off steam and behaving like boys. Relatives have since told me the pair of them were a mischievous little double act in themselves but their stepmother's stern and uncompromising behaviour somehow made them worse. On Saturday nights, for example, after a week's school they were not allowed out. It was a form of domestic repression which was bound, sooner or later, to cause a reaction so it was, in retrospect, hardly surprising that when their stepmother hid their boots one weekend to ensure they stayed at home, my father and his brother engineered an elaborate strategy of escape. One engaged her in conversation while the other hunted high and low for the boots which, once found, were left in the back privy. There an assignation was made and the two of them, like fugitives on the run, made clean their escape. Having done a bunk for the whole day, however, they were afraid to return to face their stepmother's fury.

I am convinced that his early childhood had a lasting effect on the course of my father's life and on his rather carefree attitude to it. There was no strong male influence on him and consequently no-one to keep him sympathetically in check. He was vaguely reared by an enigmatic old buffer known as Uncle Harry, who had retired from some obscure business at the age of twenty-five and had spent the next fifty years staring into the flames of the enormous black kitchen range in the cottage on the Isle of Man. But apart from him it was only his rather demanding stepmother who kept my father under her thumb. When he was old enough to leave the family home it was quite natural he should rebel against this upbringing by making up for all he had missed and going slightly off the rails. My mother was fully aware of this and duly made all the allowances she could before the strain got too great.

Dad spent the bulk of his formative teenage years on the Isle of Man before coming back to Liverpool at the age of seventeen. As he got older his stepmother began to get very jealous of him. He would often tell me how he felt she was fonder of his twin brother than of him. His brother, George, eventually went off to sea leaving Dad more or less on his own in Liverpool. In the meantime the destinies of my own parents were in the process of becoming entangled. My own mother had a friend who happened to be a Manx girl and not too distantly related to my father. The two of them eventually met in church shortly after he settled in Liverpool but it was not for another four years that they started seriously courting.

My mother's background is rather less tortuous. Born in Bootle in 1914, Margaret Mary Macdonald had a fairly conventional upbringing. Her father was a clerk at the docks and her mother worked at home bringing up three boys and four girls – a task made all the harder when her father died at the age of forty two. Mum had decided quite early on in life to train as a nurse but her mother was disapproving. Several times she wrote off for the relevant papers and application forms only to see her mother throw them on the fire. 'Nursing,' she was told, 'was only for girls who had no homes.' But Mum persisted and trained for three years at Ormskirk and Walton. Eventually she won her mother round to the idea and, in the end, earned her admiration for sticking to her guns. Nursing in those days, however, was for single women only, so when she married Dad she had to give up her career. She was twenty-six when she and he tied the knot. The date was 1940. I appeared two years later.

I am grateful to have inherited from her that streak of perseverance and determination and I respect her for being clearsighted in her ambition. Both of us have been strong willed and confident enough to make a career out of our dreams. When I was later to give up a steady job to launch myself on the uncharted seas of acting and broadcasting it was my mother who was able to understand the motivation. Paradoxically enough it was my father, the unpredictable, Bohemian dreamer, who found it hard to accept that what I was doing had a point to it. Although he came round later on when I was obviously making a go of things, it was he, above all people, who urged me not to be 'so damn stupid' and to stay put in a secure job at the docks.

All this was further proof of the two opposites which had come together in what, from an outsider's point of view, must have seemed an unlikely marriage. Surely they *must* have married for a bet! As my Dad busied himself around town, Mum would stay at home, a diligent, conscientious woman, with gnarled hands that always seemed to smell of onions. To me she seemed to be perpetually shrouded in clouds of steam and dripping washing as if Cherry Close was buried deep in the Amazonian Rain Forest.

She was a tireless and long-suffering mother to a small brood of demanding children, three in all. I am the eldest child, born in 1942; to be followed two years later by my sister, Jan, and three years after that by my brother, Don.

With Jan I felt instantly at ease. I see her now as a bright, blonde, bubbly girl shaking her curls and giggling her way through life in Cherry Close with a kind of babyfaced and compliant good humour. Nothing upset her, not even an im-promptu game I once mischievously invented when she was three. It was called, with diabolic innocence, 'Let's go to the barber's' and involved my shearing her shoulder length ringlets with a pair of scissors. As I hacked away at the golden curls Jan beamed and chortled at this exciting wheeze. When I considered the job well done I flushed the evidence down the lavatory and returned to eye my handiwork. Jan sat there, one pathetic ringlet hanging down accusingly over her right ear, still beaming. Why

Mum was in such a stinking bad temper when she returned is a mystery to me to this day.

Don was a different prospect altogether. Here was a rival. After all, we already had one boy in the family so why should we possibly want another unless he was replacement for me. This triggered off dark moods of jealousy. Had I turned out to be a useless specimen, I wondered, such a washout that they needed to supersede me with a new model? If so, I concluded, they had made a bad choice. For the first three years of his life Don seemed to do nothing else but scream. Surely this noisy midget known locally as 'the mouth in the pram' was no improvement on me even if he was brand new. It was a time of confused emotions but gradually we settled down into a relatively stable sort of coexistence with me at the head of the bizarre trio.

The fact that my mother had practised as a nurse before marrying qualified her for the role of Florence Nightingale to the family. She ministered to our childhood ailments with a series of arcane and faintly medieval remedies. Abrasions, cuts, and grazes would immediately cause the most dreaded instrument of torture in the house to be summoned – a purple, ribbed bottle, marked IODINE. This was a remedy worse than any symptom. Applied to healthy skin it was only slightly less painful than concentrated sulphuric acid but spread on an open wound it would sear through my body like stabbing knives of raw pain staining the affected part a distinctive fluorescent purple. This was reckoned to be the cure for virtually everything from tennis elbow to black death.

For many years as a child I used to wet the bed. Psychiatrists may deduce from this chronic complaint a nervous disposition, an inferiority complex, a state of semi-permanent insecurity and, who knows, they may be right. Either way the result was damp sheets up to the age of about thirteen. When maternal remedies failed to do the trick my mother would seek a second opinion from neighbours or moustachioed aunts who between them would concoct outlandish cures which invariably fell far short of their intended result.

The most eccentric of them all involved a tennis ball attached to two pieces of string. At night time shortly before I was due to retire the ball would be placed in the small of my back and the string tied together at the front. Most kids were given cocoa and biscuits and had a fairy tale read to them before bedtime. I had a tennis ball tied round my middle. Perhaps you can understand now why I thought our household faintly odd.

The theory behind this primitive device was of such cunning simplicity that it would have astonished the Pharaohs. Bed wetting took place, according to the Cherry Close Medical Council, only when I was sleeping on my back. Were I inclined to roll over in the night the sensation of the tennis ball, causing acute curvature of the spine, would wake me up. I, in turn, thankful for the early warning device would rise and make my way to the lavatory to answer Nature's call.

In practice of course we could never tie the strings tight enough and it would ride round to the front so that by the time the dawn came I would once again be lying in a cold and mossy patch of bedlinen. The tennis ball meanwhile would be hanging limply somewhere near my navel like a tired pom-pom lending me the appearance of a midget Pierrot slightly the worse for wear.

The second futile cure for this socially embarrassing childhood complaint came via a toothless harridan who would turn up at the house periodically from her lair in Anfield. This latest rigmarole required one to shape a sheet of paper into a funnel down which a mysterious white powder would be poured. A third party was then recruited, usually my mother, who was then supposed to aim the contraption at my open mouth and blow the magic dust down my throat. Whether this was meant to be a bona fide cure for bed wetting or a simple ruse to keep us out of mischief on a winter's night I still do not know to this day.

On the first attempt to administer the cure-all the inevitable happened. I sneezed and sent the powder back up the cylinder into Mum's face. The result: a bout of coughing and sneezing, and white faces all round as the clouds of dust filled the room. It was never tried again. I probably wet the bed laughing that night.

During all this time, of course, I was listening fanatically to the radio. I even bought my own copy of the Radio Times to make sure I missed nothing that was broadcast. It was more than a hobby or a passing childish interest. It was a passion – all consuming, all embracing and a solace in my early childhood.

A poignant moment I recall was in 1948, a small incident really, but in its minor way deeply saddening. By this time I was a regular listener to the BBC, a fan, although I imagine that word did not exist then either, of the legendary radio men, John Snagge, Stuart Hibberd, Bruce Wyndham, Alvar Liddell. It was a Saturday morning and I, as usual, was camped by the wireless listening not so much to the races or the news as to the *voices*. It was those wonderful announcers who gripped my imagination. I would sit there picturing Kenneth Wolstenholme at the microphone wearing his headphones and commenting on a race or a match. In my innocence, I imagined there was a finite number of microphones at Broadcasting House and that if I did not work fast that supply would be exhausted by the time I grew up. 'I hope there are enough microphones left by the time I get to London, Dad,' I would say in all sincerity. Dad used to work at the undertaker's on Saturday until midday, so I would listen to the radio in the morning and go out to the end of the close at dinner time to wait for him to come home. He, however, would often go straight to the Hermitage after work and was bound for a long session. I waited and waited at the end of the close,

I join the Scouts

A Scouting expedition to Tawd
Vale, Liverpool in 1953

On the way to the Isle of Man, 1957

Rowing in Port St Mary Bay, Isle
of Man

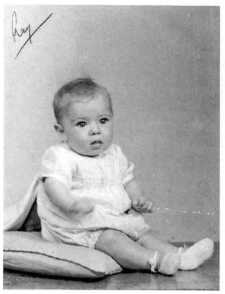

My first photograph, 1942

Southport, 1949. Cycling was an early passion

With my brother in 1951 at Ainsdale

The school boy, 1952

Above: My parents, Isle of
Man, 1956. *Right*: Oldham
Repertory, 1961. A James
Dean look-alike

Left: Publicity photo sent out to unsuspecting theatrical impresarios, 1962. *Below*: Sidmouth Repertory Theatre, 1962

A BBC publicity photo shortly after I arrived in London, 1967

In front of the microphone at last, 1968

Left: Alma and I on honeymoon, 1969. *Below*: With some admirers. Night Ride, 1969

Caption to precede and tail Granada evening newscast

peering down the road for a sign of Dad, wondering where he was and desperate to tell him what I had been listening to on the radio that day. But still he did not appear. It began to go dark and Mum came out to fetch me in for tea. Then it was bed time and still he did not show.

But he loved us all. It was simply that he never grew up. He was still the lad from the Isle of Man ready to bunk off for the day and let off steam.

When he was at home he was marvellous company with a never ending string of stories to keep the whole house red-eyed with laughter. He never tired of talking of his exotic relations across the water where, it seemed to us, everybody was related in some way with assorted Quayles, Mylchreests, Kinveigs and Shimmins, forever in and out of their family cottage on the Isle of Man. There was a fisherman called Daniel Christian who sported a long flowing beard and whose sepia portrait adorned the parlour wall. This ancient and venerable relative, we were told, was the actual model for the crusty old salt pictured on the lid of Skipper sardines. So our family could lay claim to immortality after all. Our relative – like the sardines – was preserved in oils.

Another tenuous relation, we were told, was a delightful rogue, with the unlikely name of Paddy Haddock, who, at an early age, had emigrated to Australia and was believed to have struck gold. Many years later he returned to his humble origins driving a Rolls Royce and parading an actress he claimed to be his wife. He had also undergone a change of identity. Paddy Haddock, for some reason best known to himself had become Sheffield Qualtrough and was by now quite mad. This was nothing new. Many of Dad's contemporaries on the island would seem a bit potty by today's standards. Billy Cregeen, for instance, a tubby, ruddy faced man who giggled incessantly at private unspoken jokes. Here was a world which owed as much to the pages of Thomas Hardy as it did to the cartoons of Film Fun. Billy's role in life was to shuffle round the farms with his broken down horse and cart dispensing paraffin oil. After many years eking out this tenuous living Billy's whole being exuded the heavy aroma of paraffin. In chapel on Sunday the congregation knew before entering if Billy was at his devotions. Once at a picture house in Port Erin the pong of paraffin on him was so strong that the manager had him chucked out on the grounds that he was a fire risk.

It was from this menagerie of eccentrics that my Dad escaped, before settling into the comparatively genteel surroundings of Liverpool.

But he came equipped with many of the inherited oddities of his lineage. In those days he consumed inordinate quantities of onions and, while peeling them, always wore a pair of goggles. Whenever I entered the kitchen on such occasions it seemed to me that Captain Biggles himself was busy preparing dinner. These goggles were always referred to as his 'onion glasses'. I remember one Christmas deciding to buy him a new pair so I scoured every shop in Liverpool to find them, asking assistant after assistant for a nice pair of onion glasses for my Dad. Each time I was met with blank stares or sympathetic giggles as they assumed the glasses to be generically related to sky hooks, elbow grease and tartan paint. It was an endearing characteristic of my father's that the world he inhabited as an everyday reality was often viewed by others as a sort of surreal, imaginative fiction. He saw the world through child's eyes and I could not help but love him for it.

The simplest thing was transformed in his hands into an object of wonder. Dad used to go to work on a bike at this time – a curious cast iron affair which weighed as much as a medium sized battleship. It sported a pair of drop handlebars which, instead of drooping downwards, Dad had arranged to point upwards. After a convivial Saturday lunchtime session in The Hermitage he would come wheeling and hiccoughing unsteadily along Cherry Close as though he were astride some mechanical bucking bronco.

We often used to go on cycle trips together to Chester, or Ormskirk or even to the alien territory of Southport on day long excursions which made me feel very close to him. Once, coming back from Old Swan he suddenly keeled off the bike in a sideways swoon like a great felled ox. 'It's the dratted cramp', he yelled, 'Grip it! My leg. Grip it!' He believed that the sovereign cure for cramp was to roll up his trouser leg and for some ministering angel to squeeze the affected part. I, meanwhile, was convulsed with hysterics which only inflamed him more, 'Grip it, grip it, y'blithering idiot!' We must have presented an unusual sight to the straight laced burghers of Old Swan – one great man squirming in agony in the road and one small boy writhing in hilarity on the pavement. Life with Dad was never dull.

He was a cabinet maker with a firm of undertakers and would be allowed from time to time to bring the hearse home with him. By now, of course, the neighbours were used to this threatening vehicle parked outside No.2. The high spot for me was when he drove me back to school in it the next morning. It had the lovely smell of petrol and old leather. He would sit grandly at the wheel in Homburg and overcoat while my nose and peaked cap barely cleared the dashboard.

As we arrived at the playground, activity would come to a halt as the kids swarmed around him pleading to be given a ride in this great black mobile mausoleum. 'Go on, Mister. You'd get fifty of us in there, easy.' No one – least of all my Dad – saw anything odd about giving someone a ride in the hearse. But even he drew the line at letting a classful of runny-nosed kids climb into its spotless interior. 'A bit of respect for the dead, boys', would be his standard reply as he pulled nonchalantly away.

The school itself was the Florence Melly School which, predictably enough, caused all of us who attended it to be known for ever more as the 'Florence Smellies'.

Although Dad was a talented carpenter all his efforts around the house had a lumpen quality about them. A brutish set of bedside drawers made of solid, untreated mahogany required feats of Herculean strength to open. If you needed a clean shirt it was advisable to start yanking and heaving at least an hour in advance. Dad was responsible, too, for a peculiar wardrobe which seemed capable of independent life. Most of the time it lolled indifferently in an alcove but the slightest touch on any of the doors would cause it to lurch uncontrollably sideways and deposit all its contents in a ragged heap by your feet. Even my long-suffering mother would hurl violent abuse at the thing, 'Another damned, cheap-jack, botch-up of your father's.'

But there were more demanding eccentricities than his efforts at home carpentry – and these Mum bore with resignation. Frequently he was away socialising most of the day and half of the night. When he did return, contrite and rheumy eyed, he would come bearing gifts of conciliation – flowers and chocolates for Mum and Dinky toys for me. I loved these occasions. But one look at him and at his bedraggled gifts was enough to infuriate Mum to near breaking point. Immediate hostilities may have temporarily ceased but a state of armed neutrality would descend on the house often lasting for days. All I remember about the rows and the arguments was a certain perverse excitement surrounding it all. A feeling that, in the absence of a father to look after Jan and Don, I would be the one to hold the family together. The strain of all the drinking was, however, beginning to make its mark on Mum.

[36]

In many ways Dad was a tormented soul. There was some sort of Celtic connection somewhere which I think he has passed on to me. It is the influence of the great pendulum swings of mood or sudden shafts of light penetrating the gloom. When you are high, by God, you really are high and everything is right with the world, so much so that you want to drink in that experience in one great gulp. But when you are low you feel like shooting yourself. I think I am more like Dad than I ever imagined.

In the early stages Mum was tolerant. She knew he had had a very repressive life on the Isle of Man, kept under his stepmother's thumb with no male influence to lighten the discipline, and she was prepared to make allowances. When he married he was shaking off the shackles of his early childhood and making up for lost time. He was really living an adolescent's life in his thirties, going a bit wild by drinking too much and staying out late.

He was also a proud member of a sub-masonic, secret society – although it was no secret to us what its members got up to – known as The Liverpool and Manchester Half Yearly Dividing Society. This curious association clearly had pretensions to greatness because my Dad was issued with regalia which lived in a collection of brown paper parcels under the bed in the front room. Secretly I would undo these parcels and stare at this weird collection of tunics, trousers and tricorn hats, heavily decorated with gold braid and tassels.

The precise object of this society remains a mystery to us to this day but it took no brain power at all to discover that each member contributed sixpence a week to a common purse. After six months the brethren would meet in either Manchester or Liverpool and divide it. They would then proceed to drink their way through the accumulated savings – a process which could take several days. Dad would then return unsteadily up the

[37]

East Lanes Road on his bike with the cow horns like a survivor from the retreat of Moscow. He would sit in the kitchen slurping tea from a saucer explaining to my mother the real purpose, as he saw it, of these drunken wanderings: 'Lots of good business done; a cracking bunch of blokes; a fellow needs to relieve the pressure of work.' On occasions like this, the familiar state of armed neutrality would set in almost at once.

My father's love of the bottle meant a steady drain on the family finances and economies had to be made in other areas to compensate for the slow leak. His own contribution to frugality involved cobbling his own boots. This was a Sunday morning religion to him. Once a week he would be seen squatting at an old bench in the back yard sweating and cursing, and slicing layers off sheets of leather and the tops of his thumbs. With nails clenched between his teeth he would begin to hammer and bang at old boots laid before him which, once the operation was completed, he would try on for size, clumping around the yard as if he had just mastered the art of walking.

Home decorating was another of his great money-saving specialities. Mum always threatened to get 'a proper man' in to do the job but Dad would have none of it. His preferred technique had a curious sameness about it, arising out of an obsession with the process of 'stippling'. Nobody stipples now-adays – I don't think anybody did then, to be honest – but Dad stippled everything. The technique involved patting the wall with a round headed paintbrush in order to give the surface a dappled look. Subtlety was the guiding principle if the technique was to have its desired effect. But subtlety was not known to be one of Dad's strongest suits and often the walls and ceiling would look as though we had had a plague of cockroaches in muddy boots tearing through the place.

One evening my father came home after a heavy day's work. A heavy day for him involved attending funerals (and the receptions afterwards) and in particular Catholic wakes. A wake would have him somewhat starry-eyed by four o'clock and in this state he would arrive in The Hermitage for another quick one to set him up for the evening. It was after just such a hard day officiating at a wake that my father arrived home one evening, unexpectedly early – before The Hermitage had closed, that is. The emotions of the day were weighing heavily upon him as he swayed ponderously in the doorway. My mother, as usual, was furious, expecting him to finish the kitchen decorating that evening and concluding he was in no state to do it. She had correctly evaluated his ability to do the job but had completely misjudged his intentions. 'Of course I'll paint the kitchen', he cried obstinately. 'Why do you think I'm home so early?'

At ten o'clock my mother went to bed in a towering huff while Dad persevered with his recreation of the Sistine Chapel downstairs. Sleep was impossible with all the incessant stippling and the curses and shouts. There was some respite when he broke off for periods of refreshment from a bottle of something which he had brought back from The Hermitage and tucked into his back pocket. At gone three in the morning Dad himself finally retired. The next day Mum came down to find the kitchen stippled beyond belief. The stipple had affected the stove, the table, the chairs, windows, doors, floor; even the inside of cupboards had not escaped. It was as if the place had been struck down overnight by some pernicious Biblical plague. Jan and I giggled, Mother sobbed and Dad climbed into the hearse heading off for another hard day, toasting the memory of dear friends he had never known.

When I was born most of the other men of Dad's age were away at the war. He himself had volunteered to join the Navy, which seemed appropriate enough given his Spanish Armada background, but the Navy wanted only men who were 100% fit to get themselves killed. Their medical people had decided that a dickie heart and flat feet were enough to put Dad out of the action and he was eventually assigned the task of firewatching in the city. So he spent most of the war at home among the bombs of Liverpool doing what he was happy to call 'firewatching', but which was a convenient way of legitimately being out of the house all night, every night. I think my Dad considered that Mr Hitler was waging a one man campaign against intemperance on British licensed premises and so thought it his patriotic duty to stand up manfully to this attack. As a result he did his duty in three or four of the local pubs every evening and, by the time dawn broke, arrived home, usually with something nourishing sticking out of his coat pocket, unable to recognise Dante's Inferno at fifty yards.

The drinking was by now putting enormous stress on my mother. We kids were unaware of it, however, and to us Dad seemed just as cheerful, just as much the madcap as ever. His inventiveness knew no bounds and whenever he was around it felt as if a wizard had just materialised to mystify and entertain us with a whole series of incredible tricks. One Christmas Eve he decided to get us all making paper decorations to hang up round the house. My mother had cleared the place immaculately, doing what she called her 'serious bottoming' and we all sat round the fire while Dad and I fiddled with streamers which we had made out of scraps of newspaper. For most households this would have been decoration enough. But not for Dad. He strode off into the outside shed and reappeared with a cup of sweet-smelling, purply liquid. He told me it was something called meths which we could use to stain the streamers in beautiful technicolour patterns. The fact that he viewed the world in an almost permanent technicolour haze must have made this operation peculiarly appropriate. Once the paper had been soaked in the liquid there was then an inch or so of meths left in the cup. With an extravagant sweep of the arm he flung it on the fire. There was one almighty WHOOSH, a sheet of flame shot up the chimney, and half a ton of soot came billowing out into the room in all directions. When the dust and grime finally settled, Mum and Jan, who were nearest the pyrotechnics, looked like the original Coal Black Mammy and Piccaninni, while Dad reeled about the floor beside himself with laughter. To recover his composure, and probably to get away from my mother's temper, he went for his hat and coat and explained that he was 'just pottering down the road for a minute'.

As things got worse, though, I think even I was aware that something was not quite right at home. During the day life at the Florence Melly School was delightful enough. It was a lovely, sunny place with classrooms dotted round a grassy quadrangle where I learnt to appreciate the finer points of plasticine, and flour and water paste. But I slowly came to realise that my father's ruddy, perspiring face at the railings at four o'clock on odd afternoons would signal a tempestuous evening ahead. On our arrival home we would be greeted by my mother scowling like thunder and complaining that he was the worse for wear again. This so upset him that he turned round there and then, muttered something about going somewhere 'that gave a bloke a decent welcome', and wobbled off on his old peculiar bike like a catatonic jockey on a mechanical horse.

Over the next couple of years my Dad's passionate devotion to the licensed victualling fraternity became almost an obsession. It was like a voracious demonic force within him, propelling him on these three day binges from which he returned in some desperate states. What he did on them, where he slept, where he ate are blank unanswered questions. Much later, he did hint at the sort of existence he led – but this was a period in his life he preferred not to dwell on. It was a time which would see, for example, the sporadic removal of the contents of the house – the three piece suite, bits of jewellery – all to assuage the demon drink. We were never certain that the beds we were sleeping on would still be there when we woke up.

It was a time which Mum prefers to forget even now. The pressure was enough to drive her to the end (and beyond) of her emotional tether. The worry brought on asthma and depression and I remember once seeing her bitterly sobbing in the kitchen. At one particularly low point she was confined to her bed on doctor's orders for a month. Clearly Mum and Dad were heading for a major confrontation. The breaking point, when it came, was not the result of one cataclysmic event. It was rather the slow accumulation of pressure which became too much to bear. It was doubly hard for Mum because she loved Dad dearly. She did not want to see him go but felt it was the only solution for the sake of the children. It was a heartbreaking decision to have to make, but a separation, she felt, might give Dad the opportunity to realise how bad things had become. I cannot recall any dramatic 'your Dad's never coming back again' sort of scene, it was just that all of a sudden Dad was gone.

His departure coincided with another great event in the family's life. Moving house. By now Cherry Close was like a battery hen house, with no room at all for Jan, Don, me and Mum to spread our wings. True, there was marginally more space now that Dad had gone, but still not enough. Mum began looking for a bigger house and eventually found one five miles up the coast in a genteel suburb called Waterloo. During this transitional period while the arrangements for the removal were being made I stayed with Grandma. The house was shared by two maiden aunts (Mum's sisters) who very kindly made clothes for me. Unfortunately, since neither of my aunts seemed too familiar with the male anatomy, the coats I wore were all tailored for girls. When you are seven going on eight, determined to be a man, and to keep the family together, then the prospect of wearing girl's clothes does little to keep your dignity intact!

The three storey Victorian terraced house we finally settled in generated great excitement all round. We rented the house from an old lady called Mrs Mason who, on the evidence of the inside of the place, had a terrible phobia about soap, polish, and clean clothes. Not to put too fine a point on it, the house ponged. Despite the state of the internal decor we kids demanded to sleep there on the very first night – after all, we were not to be put off by a bit of dust and a musty smell. The place seemed enormous after Cherry Close, and we were determined to enjoy our new home – even if it did leave Mum scrubbing and cleaning away for a full three weeks before it was judged clean enough to be genuinely habitable.

As we sat on boxes and packing cases drinking cocoa, I remember the sheer exhilaration of it all. Although I missed Dad I was excited by the prospect of taking charge of the household, of looking after Don, Jan and Mum, and together embarking on a new adventure.

[3]

In many respects I now saw myself as the new head of the family. Whether riding my bike, like a circus act with Don on the handlebars and Jan on the crossbar, or going off alone to do the shopping, I felt I was in charge. I was grown up.

As I grew older, both Mum and Gran had tremendous faith in me. Gran might say, 'I want such and such a thing from Marks and Spencer's and such a such from John Lewis. Now here's a ten shilling note, get your train fare out of that and make sure you count your change. When you get into town make sure you don't pay more for anything than I've told you.' So, feeling ever so grand, I would casually remark to Don and Jan that I was 'just going off to Liverpool to do a few errands'. It was a wonderful feeling to have such responsibility at the time and to be trusted to go all that way by myself. I cannot imagine sending an eight year old into the city nowadays on his own.

By now I was a reluctant pupil at St Luke's Junior Boys' School in Crosby and, after the carefree days at Florence Melly's establishment, St Luke's was grim indeed. A crumbling Victorian edifice permanently reeking of stale bread and milk. Instead of the little grassy square to play on we now had a mean and unwelcoming patch of back yard. It was large and draughty and I seemed to be perpetually freezing cold. At the back of the school there was a working blacksmith's. These were the days when horses were regularly used for deliveries. Milkmen, draymen, coalmen, all used horses and the smithy behind us was in constant use. It emitted black plumes of acrid smoke and the most revolting stench of rotting flesh. In the summer it also attracted swarms of horseflies, the size of small birds. When stung we all came out in large blisters which resembled hard boiled eggs. Add to this the fact that many of the schoolkids wore the same clothes every day for a term and that I was still wetting the bed and you have something of an idea of the place. The combination of burning horse flesh, body odour and stale urine meant St Luke's must have been an awesome nasal experience for passers-by.

It was in this atmosphere that I attempted to learn the rudiments of grammar and sums. By way of relief from this brainwork I joined the cubs, making do with a cobbled together uniform and a homemade woggle. Its attraction for me lay in the fact that they encouraged us to fiddle about with bits of string and make fires – all the things I was never allowed to do at home. I suppose it was a way of letting off steam in a boyish way and provided something of a contrast to the adult responsibilities I was given in the house. A neighbour once came to see us and remarked casually to my mother, 'Isn't Ray old?'

At the time I could not understand why Mum so often seemed in a bad temper. Now, of course, the reason is clear. She was still under tremendous pressure to keep the family together, without a husband there to help her. For a time, it seemed to me that nothing I did could please her. I would wash the dishes but they were not quite as clean as they should be; I would wipe the kitchen floor but it was not polished quite as well as it should be. And at the end of the day I wanted a bit of praise. It always seemed to be a case of 'Why haven't you done A, B and C?' The fact that I had done D, E, F, and G, did not seem to count for anything.

I remember once saving up some money for a present for her but I did not know what to buy. So, thinking she would like to choose something for herself, I got a pound note – one of the big old ones – got a box that just fitted it and wrapped it up elaborately. When she opened it she went wild, 'Don't ever give me money', she shouted to my utter incomprehension. I understand it all now, of course, and realise she meant nothing by it. It was simply a measure of the strain she was under. All she wanted was for the home to be back to normal with Dad back with us again. In his absence the whole burden of supporting a house and three children demanded enormous physical and mental reserves and, in such circumstances, occasional outbursts were only natural.

Life was not hard all the time of course, far from it. After the cubs I graduated to the scouts which involved going away to camp for a week at a time and enjoying a glorious licence to do virtually anything . . . living on conny-onny sandwiches, climbing trees and dangling over rivers. To avoid embarrassment caused by my ever present potential for bed wetting, I forced myself to stay awake all night. By the end of the week I would arrive home dirty, gaunt-faced and tired to the point of exhaustion. Any connection our troop had with Baden Powell's high ideals was a tenuous one indeed.

At home or away my preoccupation with the BBC was growing. My life revolved round Dick Barton, Journey into Space and a wonderful northern comedy series called Clubnight, which involved a Scouse character diving in and out of the action. So it was possible to be from Liverpool *and* be on the radio!

In those days I made no distinction between light entertainment and newsreading – it was all radio and I loved every moment of it. And yet it was the announcers I revered most – John Snagge, Stuart Hibberd, Joy Worth, Michael Brooke were all gods to me. But there seemed to be this unbridgeable gulf between their world and mine. I wrote fan letters to them and waited in agony for them to reply. I once asked Stuart Hibberd how I could become an announcer. He wrote back to say that he thought a good education was the first thing to get. Having half-expected him to send me a return railway ticket to London and a personal tour round the studios of Broadcasting House I was most disappointed with this limp response. When I was later to meet him in the announcers' room at the BBC, I was careful to conceal my boyish disappointment.

In 1951 the opportunity to get close to the object of my dreams came within my grasp. There was an official St Luke's day trip to London to see the Festival of Britain. My plan was to get to London, give the Festival of Britain a miss (I was not at all sure what it was anyway) and head up Regent Street to see Broadcasting House for real. It seemed the most exciting idea in the world, carrying as it did the possibility of catching a glimpse of one of my heroes. There was only one drawback. The price of the adventure was 12s 6d per boy and with Dad still missing that amounted to a ridiculous fortune to go frittering away on a day's gallivanting to London. The rest of St Luke's went and I was given the day off. I listened to the radio and imagined, through my tears, that I could actually have been in the very place where these lovely voices were coming from.

At this time my mother was determined that none of us would follow my father down his particular road to perdition and, as a protection from temptation, we were fed a hefty diet of religion. Sundays were exhausting. A Scottish Presbyterian Church in the morning, a Baptist Sunday school in the afternoon and a Seaman's Mission Tin Tabernacle in the evening. It began to be confusing. My Gran, a wonderful, warm, compassionate woman, summed it all up when she told us, 'Going to church is a religion with your mother.'

On one of these Sunday mornings in church I suddenly bent double in agony with stomach pains and was carted off home like a broken stick. The next minute I was in Alder Hey Children's Hospital undergoing an emergency appendix operation. Many years later the great scriptwriter, Eddie Braben, who still lives near the hospital, said, when I told him the Alder Hey was where I had my appendix removed, 'Oh, so that's what was hanging on the gate!' I was in the hospital at the time of the Coronation and I listened to the coverage in wonder and admiration. More legendary names were being added to my list of heroes – Godfrey Talbot, Raymond Baxter, Audrey Russell, Brian Johnston, whose commentaries far overshadowed any trivial event taking place in the Abbey.

The terms of the separation meant Dad was to have no contact with us at all except for mutually agreed periods. At the time, of course, I had no idea of this and so was constantly baffled that we could only ever see him in a windy little park by the shore, usually with my mother's fiery eyes burning through its shrubbery some distance away. He would appear, usually sober and tidy now, with cars for me and Don, and dolls for Jan. And then, all too quickly, he was gone. On occasions he used to meet us clandestinely as we came out of Sunday School. As usual he would come around with presents for us all but would add a cautionary, 'Don't tell your mother I've seen you' before leaving for goodness knew where. I always imagined he lived in some sort of kennel.

But during his five year absence from the home my father, by monumental strength of will, was fighting his way back up. And he had a long way to climb. Much later, when I was married, he used to tell me of some of the desperate lodgings he had had. Usually these were doss houses or working mens' hostels and grim places in the extreme. The main fear in these hostels was to have your boots stolen and the only way to prevent this was to stand the legs of the cast iron bedstead inside your boots at night. Any light fingered boot-fancier would then have to lift the whole bedstead, containing thirteen stone of my father's comatose frame, before successfully making off with the prize.

On another occasion, he told me, he went into the washroom one morning to spruce himself up for the day ahead, after a particularly heavy session the night before. Distractedly he reached for the soap and gave himself the Niagara-style all-over douche to which he was accustomed. Seconds later he stared in horror at the basin as blood spattered everywhere from cuts in his face and hands. What had happened was that the soap he had reached for contained a razor blade – normal practice then, to prevent so prized a possession from blunting – but Dad had not seen this because he was new to the game. When he turned up that week on the windy foreshore to see us he looked as though he had been in a dreadful fight.

At the time I dared not ask him how he had arrived in that state. Later in life I realised. Things became so bad through drink at one point, that even the Salvation Army would not take him in.

But, through sheer effort he rose back up again from the ashes. He often told us towards the end of his life that it was only the thought of Mum and us kids that kept him from going under. He loved us so much and was so heartbroken at being apart that he was determined to rehabilitate himself. By now, of course, he had been sacked from the undertaker's and had been taken on at Cammell Lairds, the shipbuilders. This meant he had more money in his pocket and could afford to move to more salubrious lodgings. It did not go unnoticed by Mum that he was now staying at better addresses and was clearly making an effort to reform.

From then on the meetings became less impersonal affairs. From time to time he would come home with us for tea and the five of us would be briefly united in a tense, uncomfortable feast of cling peaches and bread and butter. After the atmosphere had warmed a little it was time for Dad to go and he would be bundled into the darkness back to his garret in Birkenhead.

Gradually he was opening up his feelings to us and he was making it quite clear, in that sentimental and genuine way of his, that he missed us all more than he could say. I think we could see that Mum was softening. And with good reason. He had a steady job which involved hard work and regular hours at the shipyard – he used to claim he had built the Ark Royal single handed – and he was putting money aside to save. His days of frittering it away on the booze had gone. It was clear that he was beginning to redeem himself in Mum's eyes and, as if in recognition of that, there would be occasional, tentative family outings to New Brighton or Southport. He had slipped the clutches of the drink, was working day and night, and his welcome back to the fold was not long away.

He came back without announcement. I came home from school one lunchtime and there he was sitting in the kitchen. The emotions were so confused that I could not understand what was happening. Part of me was glad he was back and part of me was frightened. It was not unlike the days when he was out on the drink. Part of me then longed for him to be back home and part of me feared what sort of a state he would be in. But now he was back for good. After seeing him once a month maybe for the past five years I did not know what to make of this permanent guest who now threatened to usurp my role in the family. It was disconcerting to hear another man's voice in the morning. And if he ever raised his voice to tell Don off, I would get resentful. Don was a stubborn, pigheaded kid, I knew that, but no one had the right to tell him off, least of all this sudden stranger. I was twelve by this time and over the past five years we had all worked out a pattern of living. The arrival of another adult was disrupting all that and the effect was not pleasant. I had been the one to fetch Jan and Don from school. I had been the one to cut the privet hedge. Now here was a stranger, apparently ordering me about. Looking back, I must have been insufferable and enough to drive the poor man back to the bottle.

There were one or two lapses but he stuck to the sober life after that. By now he had learnt his lesson well and he was able to go to the pub on a Saturday night and spend an hour over a pint without the temptation of taking off on three day benders. He was always a gregarious man, fonder of the company, I am sure, than of the drink. In later life though, his world seemed to close round the family. He had had drinking companions by the score, but they had deserted him when the crunch came, and so he was left with very few close friends.

Normal family life was at last resumed and now that, for the first time I could remember, we no longer had to scrimp and scrape, it was decided we should all have a holiday together. And where else but the Isle of Man?

This was the dream my father had cherished all the time he had been away. It was the beacon towards which he had striven and whose light had sustained him through the dreary hours in those hostels in Birkenhead. He ached for the sunny days when his own children would be running through the fields where he had played as a boy.

I had not the remotest conception of what the Isle of Man could be like and naturally assumed the whole world was like Waterloo – with the damp streets, the smoky houses, and the bowling park; the swings, the duckpond, and the oily foreshore. Occasionally Sunday School picnics took us to exotic locations such as Frodsham, Thurstaston or the Botanic Gardens of Churchtown, but these places always seemed unreal and artificial. In any case, running a three legged race in Churchtown was really no more exciting than one in our own street. Uncle Alan took us in his car to the Trough of Bowland once, which was pretty enough – but festooned with irksome commandments: No Fishing; No Lighting Fires; No Climbing Trees. This 'wild open' country seemed to be more restricting than the city – at least you could *enjoy* that anarchic, tumbledown life on the street.

Now that he was sober, Dad became a meticulous man. He sent away for brochures, maps and tourist guides and began to consult timetables, gauging the most propitious time to travel. Jan, Don and I peered at the pictures in the brochures in pure wonderment. These glorious, sunlit beaches, and woodland glades, these gnarled fishermen mending nets surely belonged to a never-never land. Surely it was a pipe dream to expect to spend a fortnight there. And as the day grew closer so the dream seemed less and less likely.

I used to go down to the shoreline to watch the Isle of Man boats coming and going and then look out across the river, scanning the horizon for this mystical island of sunny faces and clean children. Standing there on Waterloo beach, amid the mud, the oil, the driftwood and the rusty bikes it was perfectly obvious to me that nowhere like the Isle of Man could possibly exist across that bit of dark threatening water. Indeed the fact that you could not see the island from our beach only confirmed my worst fears – that we were all being subjected to a cruel hoax.

But the great day finally dawned. We got up at four in the morning – as was usual practice whenever the Moore household set off 'en famille' – and climbed into a black taxi which was waiting outside. A few minutes later we were clattering along the cobbles of the Dock Road towards the landing stage. In those days the stage seemed to be about five miles long. Nowadays it is reduced to a pathetic little ramp of about three feet.

The Isle of Man boats came and went at the North end of the stage and as we approached I could see the distinctive red and black funnels and gleaming white superstructures of the boats. To me they looked like so many miniature Queen

Elizabeths. We were bundled, complete with battered suitcases, into an enormous waiting room the size of Lime Street Station, the rows of wooden seats stretching into infinity. It was packed to bursting point with grannies, babies, kids and dogs all kicking up a monumental babble of excitement and anticipation. This was, of course, high summer, so, when one boat was full, another was waiting right behind to be filled in its turn. There was much shuffling of bottoms as we gradually inched our way to the front where I remember thinking that there was no island on God's earth which could accommodate this teeming throng. I imagined us all huddled for a fortnight cheek by jowl on one tiny patch of beach.

Dad was masterminding the operation which, in short, meant bobbing up and down on a sea of heads and faces and navigating towards the man who could tell us which particular boat would be taking us on this odyssey. It turned out to be an old rust bucket of uncertain vintage which, I am sure, must have done sterling work in the Crimean War.

It was called the Victoria and had two funnels which for the whole of the journey belched out smoke and made everyone cough violently. It was like a works outing from a Sanatorium. We settled down in part of the ship Dad called Aft, doubtless calling to mind his Armada connection, and, after much bawling from the dockers and sailors, we were out in the midstream of the Mersey. There we were suddenly surrounded by gigantic passenger liners, busy, hectoring tugs, and cargo ships from impossible places, Rio de Janeiro, San Francisco, Valparaiso. Dad had made this crossing many times, though usually in the smoky ambience of the saloon bar, and this was the first time, I think, he had actually sat out on deck.

The trip was exhilarating beyond anything I had ever imagined and, once beyond the bar lightship, every trace of land disappeared. The old bucket plodded through the stinging spray of the Irish sea while Dad leaned over the railings smoking casually. He seemed to know many of the sailors on board which impressed me enormously. Eventually a buzz went round the deck that the island was in sight. We hung over the side straining our eyes towards a grey smudge, barely visible on the horizon. It looked like a mirage and even if it did turn out to be real, was it big enough to house this heaving cargo of travellers? As we got closer the grey turned to brown which in turn gave way to green and as we inched towards Douglas the whole island became a bright kaleidoscope of colours. I rubbed my eyes at the green fields, the purple heather, and the misty blue hills that stretched away on either side of us. I simply could not believe that anywhere as clean and fresh and warm as this could exist. Why, you could even see fish swimming about below the pale blue water.

After much sweating and shoving we staggered towards the bus station, part of a noisy desperate tribe of refugees, all intent on the same thing. The journey to Port Erin lasted over an hour, thanks to the Manx custom of stopping the bus every five hundred yards to enable the conductor to pass the time of day with strollers and cottage dwellers, leaning over their gates in expectation of the latest gossip from the town. I looked out of the window, in increasing disbelief, at tidy fields and leafy lanes, so cosy that the branches of the trees tickled the windows of the bus as we passed. And as always the sea seemed to follow us everywhere. Around every bend it was there again, clear and sparkling beyond the lush green hills. Liverpool could not possibly exist on the same planet as this. Dad began pointing out landmarks. 'We're just coming to Aunt Essie's house; that's Uncle John's garage; this is where the Kinveig girls used to live.' I began to picture an army of unknown relatives suddenly besieging us.

We were booked into a tiny boarding house by the Four

Roads in Port St Mary. It was a very prim and shiny place which smelt of Mansion polish. At tea that night all five of us sat round a beautifully laid dining table bearing more cutlery than I had ever seen before. We three kids were told to behave and so ate our meal in a state of tense apprehension, lest any of us dropped our bread or spilt some milk. 'Please God,' I murmured, sipping my tea with exaggerated care, 'don't let it be me!'

After tea Dad suggested a walk and a visit to Gran and Uncle Harry, two characters baffling beyond belief. I could not work out who they were, still less why we should take the trouble to go and see them. I knew that Gran was not Dad's real mother and Uncle Harry was certainly not *my* uncle, so where had these imposters come from? I viewed this meeting with some nervousness.

We set off up the lane past the school my Dad had attended as a boy and I wondered how anybody could possibly go to school in a place as beautiful as this. A school was a crumbling pile like St Luke's, nothing so wonderful as this schoolhouse standing in the middle of an open field, surrounded by purple hills and foaming sea. We wandered through Rushen church-yard and every other gravestone seemed to record the death of another Moore. I came to the conclusion that the family was cursed with some terrible jinx. On the evidence of the church-yard it was amazing that any of us had survived at all.

This was indeed the stuff of dreams. Hedgerows bursting with blackberries, tumbling streams whose water tasted sweet and cool, trees laden heavily with rosy apples. At one cottage along our way, a woman in a pinny shouted, 'Across again, eh, Willie?' My Dad preened, 'Yeah, got the family here this time.' Don and I began to giggle. Why on earth should she call him Willie? I was convinced that the whole thing was a figment of my overworked imagination. A strange land where my father was suddenly known as Willie, a land populated by anonymous relations, many of whom seemed to have come to a sticky end in Rushen graveyard, must surely have existed only in my head.

Granny's cottage, standing alone among fields, was the sort of thing you see in calendars of 'Glorious Britain'. Inside it smelled warm and welcoming, with the distinctive aroma of old wood and paraffin oil. Granny used to yank away laboriously at an old hand pump in the kitchen. There was no piped water – nor any electricity. As the twilight turned to dusk, she lit several smoky paraffin lamps which I thought exciting, but rather ghostly too. We seemed to be part of an English period film – a single frame of a black and white Ealing motion picture. Uncle Harry sat in the parlour, engulfed in a large armchair beside the black, smoking range, his white hair and handlebar moustache lending him a venerable presence. He clearly did not approve of children since all our piping questions were answered with a series of incomprehensible grunts.

So we settled down, by the light of a flickering lamp, to a cosy supper of bread, which Granny had baked that morning, butter and cheese which Uncle Harry had brought from the farm down the lane, tomatoes the size of beetroots and pickled onions. Never had I tasted anything as sumptuous as this. Jan, Don and I scavenged our way across the table like locusts and then, heavy with food and a voluptuous sense of weariness, we walked out into the lane to find ourselves lost in a sea of black. The darkness, rich, sweet and velvety, was almost tangible. Then we looked up, saw the heavens teeming with millions of stars and it was as if Dad had been stippling the sky.

Don began to cry as we walked through the darkened graveyard and Dad told us tales of people being eaten alive by the great Black Dog of Surby.

Those sunny days on the island went by cruelly fast. The rowing boats in the bay, the strawberry teas in Rushen Abbey, the bikes we had hired to tear down Fishers Hill at a hundred miles an hour, the games we had played on Bradda Hill, tumbling down the heather, shrieking and calling – it was as close to Paradise as I could imagine. And most satisfying of all was to see Mum and Dad, a few paces ahead of us in the lanes, holding hands and back together again. It was a great, great joy to be united as a warm stable family. Now, at last, the circle was complete.

We returned home on an afternoon boat from Douglas and ploughed our way up the murky oily waters of the Mersey estuary as dusk fell. Liverpool looked so shabby and unkempt on that summer's evening. When we got back home to Waterloo, to the privet hedge, the bin in the back yard and the kids playing hopscotch, I went upstairs, hung out of the bathroom window and stared out west towards the setting sun in the hope that just for an instant I might catch one more glimpse of that blissful island. I saw little through my tears – only a dog below me in the entry cocking its leg against a lamp-post.

Life eventually resumed its normal course, although complete normality was never to be a feature of our curious household. Dad's sense of the ridiculous never deserted him, even though he was by now a completely changed man in all other respects. Wild and impractical schemes abounded, grand plans were laid. The first was to construct a shed in the yard to house the wellies, boots, bikes and hockey sticks which were filling the house as the family grew up. An 'L' shaped formation was decided on, so as to enable it to be neatly positioned in the corner of the yard. From the start it had a basic design fault. The roof sloped towards the yard walls causing accumulated rainwater to drain down the inside of the shed. No amount of persuasion from Don and me could change Dad's mind about this arrangement, with the result that, summer and winter, the hut was sodden.

Lush green moss began to clothe the walls as the place began to resemble the inside of a kettle slowly being furred up.

Dad installed a vice on the workbench which overnight seized up with rust. On one occasion, Jan was inside and felt the overwhelming urge to open a tin of glue called, I think, Croid. Like everything else, it was caked in rust and the lid was practically welded to the tin. In a stroke of genius she decided to loosen the lid with several blows from a rusty hammer lying nearby. It was hardly a precision tool for the job so a couple of ill judged blows ensured that the lid came off with a bang and the contents found themselves adhering randomly to every available surface. On top of this I used to use the shed on Saturday mornings to mix chemicals to produce foul smells, which meant that the whole place was a foetid health risk, to be approached with great care and only with the appropriate protection.

The shed, however, was instrumental in teaching me the facts of life in their most rudimentary form. The day marked down for this illumination coincided with a long planned operation to re-felt the roof. A strong wind was blowing up, causing the felt to flap like a loose sail in our faces. As Dad wrestled with the felt and tried to nail it to the wooden frame, he suddenly asked above the gale, 'How old are you, now, son?'

'Fourteen', I said.

'Well, you probably want to know where you came from.' I blushed a little and said I was pretty sure I knew. Mum had told me it was Parkhurst Nursing Home.

'No, no. Before that, you twerp,' he blustered and proceeded to spell out each fact of life to the accompaniment of hammer blows on the shed roof. I learnt very little from the exercise, except to form the impression that procreation must be a very violent, tempestuous business.

Dad's sense of fun was infectious and Don and I certainly caught it. After lunch on Sundays Dad regularly went upstairs for a couple of hours' snooze. Quite frequently a Salvation Army band used to parade at the end of the road and, on several occasions, Don and I would approach the Captain in charge and explain that there was a very sick man down the road who would like nothing better than to hear the band play beneath his window. The whole cavalcade would then take a detour to our house and strike up with 'Blessed Assurance' at pain level. In no time my father's purple face would appear at the window mouthing comments which were probably best left unheard and gesticulating wildly at the band who seemed confused by this odd response to their kindness.

Stage three of my education was now underway as I graduated to Waterloo Grammar School and began plodding stoically through declensions, conjugations and calculus. I was beginning to think more clearly about what I should do in life. Of course, it had to be radio. The main priority, if I was ever to be even allowed inside Broadcasting House, was to get rid of my thick Scouse accent. At about the age of seventeen I enrolled for elocution lessons with a legendary character by the name of Mrs Harold Ackerley, who occupied a curious fin de siècle salon on the third floor of Cranes buildings in Liverpool. She was a woman of formidable presence, much given to frocks with floral prints. Fingers, wrists and neck were swathed in jewellery and she seemed to rattle a lot. Of uncertain years, she wore thick lemonade bottle spectacles, which were in themselves a tribute to her eyesight, since to see anything through them would have counted as a triumph. She also chain smoked Craven A cigarettes, so that each lesson was conducted through a dense, choking fug. With her myopia and the pall of smoke she could not have known half the time whether I was in the room or not. After one hour a week of this pantomime, I came away 'enunciating beautifully', very much, or so I thought, in the clipped manner of David Niven.

'Talking posh' in Liverpool, however, was a risky undertaking and I knew how resentful Scousers could be if they felt you were getting a little above yourself. As a result, in everyday speech, I would consciously revert to sounding like a Breck Road docker although I was secretly determined to master the art of good pronunciation. After all, was this not the passport to where I wanted to be?

One of my treasured possessions of the time was a radio my Dad had bought me when he came back home. It was a lovely wooden affair which came on when you opened the lid and, most precious of all, it belonged to me alone. Both parents could see I was serious about wanting to get into broadcasting but Dad always tried his best to discourage me. After the sacrifices he had made to work hard and get himself off the drink to do the best for us, he felt that my getting involved in something as trivial as the radio would be a slap in the face. Why didn't I want a proper job?

To me, of course, this was not a job at all, it was a vocation. The urge to work in radio had come unexpectedly and unbidden. It owed nothing to my family or, really, to me. It was simply a call from outside which found an echo deep within me. I could not resist it. My ambition was finally made public at a careers lecture in my last term at the Waterloo Grammar School. The headmaster, goaded into delirium by my indifference to the glittering prizes to be won in the Civil Service, teaching and banking, finally sighed, 'All right then, Moore, what would you really like to do?'

'Read the news on the BBC, sir', I said. He snorted and laughed at this preposterous idea, while I thought to myself 'Right, son, you wait! You just wait!'.

[4]

The Dock Road in Liverpool is not the most obvious route to Broadcasting House. But that is where my journey started. That, too, was the scene of a second moment of illumination which was to dictate the course of my adult career. If the first moment in the darkened room with the bakelite wireless told me what I had to do, my experiences at the Docks told me how I would have to go about it.

I left school in the summer of 1960, unaware that I was now officially living in exciting times. The Sixties had not yet formally been termed 'Swinging' but the day was not far off. While my near-contemporaries were launching themselves into a fabulous world of success, freedom and celebrity as models, photographers, clothes designers, and boutique owners, I was starting out as a cotton sampler on the Docks. True, it was a temporary measure to fill that uncertain and seemingly interminable time between leaving school and receiving the 'A' Level results but, with no future prospect immediately in view, it took on a semi-permanence which was not entirely unappealing. Part of me rather liked this life in the docks for the contrast it provided. The work was dull but the company appealing.

The job to which I had been assigned was routine and unimaginative and involved breaking open the iron bands round the cotton bales with an axe and then fumbling around the raw cotton for a fistful of this precious commodity to send off in a cardboard box to the milltowns of Lancashire. It was tough, physical work, which left the mind untouched. I had mastered the technique within the first few hours of arrival at the docks and by lunchtime I was as skilled a cotton sampler as I could ever hope to be if I stayed in the job until I retired. Many men did, of course, and I respected them for it but it was clearly no long term job for me.

And yet, for all that, I admired this world into which I had, for the time being, been deposited. The teeming, chaotic life which the boats seemed to generate appealed to me. In those days ships used to queue up for berthing spaces; nowadays they can pretty well choose the space they want. It was a hard-nosed world that could have come straight out of the pages of Damon Runyan. There were arguments and fistfights, there was boozing and gambling and the whole place gave off the whiff of confident masculinity.

But I enjoyed the contrast between this and the rather sheltered life I had led so far. At that time in my life, in common with many an adolescent, I suppose, I was unsure of myself, unsure about who I was and what I would eventually be doing. But here were hard drinking, physically strong men who exuded a confidence in their place in the world which was as watertight as the ships they unloaded. They may have developed slow leaks as they grew older but they struck me then as enviably self-assured. I admired their raw honesty and complete lack of pretence.

I never wanted to be a lasting part of their world but to be, for a time, in their company was invigorating. Their humour and verbal inventiveness delighted me. Everybody was given a nickname on the docks and elaborate phrases which were coined charm me as much now as they did then. There was 'The Submarine', for example, given to a man who was forever saying, 'I'll be down below if you want me' – 'down below' meaning anywhere out of sight and beyond the reach of any work which might, inadvertently, come his way. Then there was 'The Baldy

Rabbit'. This was given to a docker who had the infuriating habit of forever cadging money for his bus journey home. With his flat Scouse accent his regular and tedious appeals always came out as, 'Lend me some money, will you, I've lost me fur!'

They were inventive in other ways, too. Each morning the lads would gather in a great mob by the dock gates and the foreman would pick out the lucky few he wanted for work that day. The chosen men would then form up into gangs of about sixteen. Eight of these would immediately go off to breakfast which generally took a leisurely sixty minutes, while the other eight got down to an hour's desultory work. Then the roles would be reversed so that by the end of the day something less than four hours' work would have been done by each man. A brilliantly simple idea.

The dockers were scrupulous in protecting the cargoes they unloaded. At least, that was their story. Cotton, for instance, was useless when wet. So, as the bales were hoisted out of the ship's hold, amateur meteorologists were hastily consulted for a professional (and binding) opinion. Rain would be confidently forecast on the evidence of a small patch of dark cloud no bigger than a man's hand on the edge of the horizon, and work would stop. The hatches would go on and men who had, hitherto, been aimlessly shambling around the quayside pursuing business of their own sensed a collective movement and joined it. A vast body of men would scamper off, united in this common purpose of protecting the cargo from impending damage, and gather solicitously in the myriad pubs which lined the Dock Road. Here they would congratulate themselves on their foresight and judgement. The cargo was safe. 'Another pint, George.'

The other ruse, if rain was threatened, was to go to the foreman and demand 'Wet money'. On payment of this, they might be persuaded to work faster and beat the shower. This meant superhuman activity of a kind not habitually witnessed in this part of the world and it demanded extra cash. Negotiations and squabbles were part of the daily life of the docks and when they could not be settled on the spot the cry would go up, 'Right, lads. That's it. Everybody off the job!' A Gadarene rush would then begin as the docks were emptied in an instant and further negotiations got underway, to the accompaniment of clinking glasses, in a hundred saloon bars not far away.

The purpose of my being in the docks was to earn a bit of money to run a motorbike and fuel a modest social life independent of my parents. But for the time I was there I enjoyed the experience as a way of opening doors to a world I had not known existed. Occasionally I would go out drinking with the men but I was clearly considered something of an outsider since I had a bit of an education and talked a bit 'posher' than they did. I palled up with a couple of the rough diamond types whose stories of behind the scenes activity at the docks made my hair stand on end. There is a well-known Liverpool gag which tells of a docker walking out through the gates staggering under the weight of an enormous bale of cotton which he is carrying on his shoulder. As he gets to the gate he sees a policeman who stops him and asks what he is doing with it. 'Earache', the docker replies and carries on. From the stories I heard there was more than a little truth in that joke. Many a time one or two of the men, in cahoots with a few policemen, were able to slip goods out unnoticed, while the law turned its blind eye to the goings on, in return for a small consideration.

Ships laden with fruit from California were very popular arrivals on the docks. For a long time it amazed me that those operating the cranes, normally so precise at their craft, would drop cases of fruit heavily on the quayside. Although the tins would be intact many would be buckled and twisted. They were immediately declared 'damaged cargo' and therefore useless; suitable only for stuffing in your pockets. Scurvy was a very rare complaint on the Dock Road. Those days have gone for good now. In just over twenty-five years the men and the ships have all gone. Stan Waters Cocoa Rooms, a meeting point that bustled with vibrancy and energy, is now transformed into what seems to me a forlorn cocktail lounge and the Dock Road is a mean, lonely, windswept place.

My plan at the time, although I think I secretly hoped it would not be fulfilled, was to get a place at the London School of Economics to read Politics or Philosophy. If you wanted to go there you had to put them first in your list of priorities by turning down all other university offers. When the 'A' Level results came through I had failed to get the appropriate grades for the LSE and, having burnt my boats with the other places of study, was left with nowhere to go. I needed a job.

My aunt's friend-of-a-friend who had wangled me the job of cotton sampler again came to the rescue, although it was hardly being rescued at all. It was more like a drowning man being suddenly knocked senseless by a blow from a well intentioned lifebelt and if this was the rescue, I thought, it might be preferable to sink. From being a labourer on the quayside I was undeservedly elevated to the status of the white collar and appointed Checking Clerk with the Mersey Docks and Harbour Board. This was a thousand times more draining than my work before and equalled in greyness what the docker's world had had in colour and vitality. Worse still, this job could be for life, not a temporary interlude.

The job involved a full eight hours a day checking whether the tonnages of cargo unloaded on the quayside tallied with the amounts listed in the ships' manifests. At first I failed to see why this was important – after all, how could loads of pig iron or timber simply evaporate during a voyage? Then I called to mind the cans of pineapples dropped heavily on the docks, the bales of cotton spirited away into waiting vans, and realised it was a very important job indeed. It was just such a pity that I had to do it. The banality and the repetition of it all numbed the mind and chilled the heart, driving me, in the vernacular appropriate to the job itself, bananas.

The checking department was on the fourth floor in the Dock Board building on the pierhead and we clerks sat at high Dickensian desks, perched on tall stools. Computers and even adding machines were the stuff of science fiction then, so the checking involved adding up enormous foolscap lists of tonnages in your head. The grim business commenced at nine. We would then slave away at these numbers for hours and hours on end, sharpening a pencil here, filling a pen there, until it seemed that we had spent half a lifetime chained to our desks. Then we would look up at the clock for a sign that this torment was at an end. Invariably the clock said twenty past nine. I craved the arrival of the tea trolley to bring a touch of the unexpected into this blank, uniform day. I longed for someone to drop a pencil to allow my body transitory release from my constantly hunched posture over the acreages of ledger. A visit to the lavatory was an excursion to be savoured, a moment to be planned and executed with all the determination of an army captain in wartime, plotting his escape by vaulting horse from his oppress- ive Nazi captors. When lunchtime eventually came, I shot out of the building to the pierhead, mentally shaking the sand out of my trouserlegs, and glad to be breathing the air of freedom.

Here, briefly, I had the chance to imagine worlds beyond the confines of the checking department. The Empress of Canada, the Corinthia, or the Sylvania were tied up there, bound for New York or Montreal while, out on the river, cargo boats steamed past me from Shanghai or Rangoon. The checking department was grimmer than ever in the afternoon. The only dismal highlight was the odd day when one or two of us would be let out on the wages run, touring all the docks and handing out little brown envelopes with transparent windows for viewing the pound notes they contained. One of our stops was the Birkenhead Chain Works, a place not even my most fevered nightmares could have portrayed. This was Hell itself. Black, oily and ringing to the uninterrupted, deafening clang of metal on metal, it was entered through a small hatch in a colossal steel door. 'Abandon all hope, ye who enter here', could have been the legend above the portal. All it actually said was, 'Mind your head'. Being there physically frightened me. The noise was painful and the picture of human beings scurrying about among this mayhem like extras in Fritz Lang's 'Metropolis' depressed me beyond belief. What is more, there was never a chain in sight. It seemed like a furious treadmill that led to nowhere. It also frightened me for another reason. In its overdramatised way the Birkenhead Chain Works was the nightmarish representation of the rest of my life if I did not act quickly to change it. By now I had been at the Dock Board for six months and my life was leading nowhere.

One morning, on the train to work, I was suddenly seized by a revolutionary idea. It dawned on me that at the age of nineteen, with no ties and no responsibilities, I could, if I wished, do *anything*. Hop on one of the ships, go to Auckland or join the circus, *anything*. Without knowing exactly what I might do I went to the Dock Board and gave them a month's notice. I told no-one, least of all Mum and Dad, who were quietly pleased I had landed such a stable job with prospects.

For a reason I cannot explain I had an obsession with time and almost a premonition that I would not get long. I had to move fast. Even the possibility of going to university seemed to slow up the process of getting where I wanted. The BBC was the goal and I felt that three years studying would set me back by three years rather than take me on towards it. At that time an Oxbridge background or a 'good war' were the classic qualifications for entry, so a scallywag like me had little hope of getting in, in one. I had to work for it.

And so I considered the two secondary routes; journalism or the theatre. If I wanted to be on the air, emulating my great heroes, the first thing I would have to correct was my Scouse accent. Mrs Harold Ackerley had done her bit but much more was needed. If I could get away from Liverpool, I thought, and move into the theatre, then at least I would be among people who spoke properly. I could learn from them. And, what was more, I would be surrounded by people who themselves would have been on the radio or television.

The Radio Times gave way to 'The Stage' as regular and required reading as I combed the Sits. Vac. columns for my big chance. I landed a job, eventually, at Oldham Repertory Theatre, where I was to be taken on as a very junior ASM – an assistant stage manager or all purpose dogsbody. I quit the Dock Board on Friday and started in Oldham on Monday.

The news hit my father like a medicine ball in the solar plexus. It was an utter repudiation of all he had worked for; two fingers waved defiantly in the face of a man who had pulled himself up from the gutter to help give us a good education and the chance of a secure job. He had fought a spectacular struggle with himself and the bottle, reformed and redeemed himself, had worked days and nights to provide for us and for what? To see his son 'gallivanting off with a troupe of rogues and vagabonds'. My mother offered me her support and succeeded in making relations between Dad and me just tolerable but he was never won over to the idea. The whole thing struck him as ludicrous and shameful by turns. I tried to explain that this was merely a stepping stone to a secure job with the BBC, but the notion that I would one day be reading the news he considered even more preposterous. A job as a teacher or a civil servant or some kind of manager at the Dock Board were the only forms of

[68]

employment he was prepared to countenance. Treading the boards was an occupation as exotic as treading grapes as far as he was concerned – and not half as acceptable.

Setting out that Sunday afternoon was like embarking on a journey of epic proportions. Oldham was all of forty miles away but it could have been on the other side of the Equator. Waterloo was hardly a sophisticated cosmopolitan centre but Oldham sounded a genuinely flat-footed and dim-witted sort of place. At the time Scousers considered London to be Britain's second city, so a little known Lancashire town up country was going to have little appeal to the likes of me.

I arrived in a suburb of Oldham called Mumps – its name was the only infectious thing about it – and it was as if I had stepped into a Lowry painting he had decided to execute in black and white. It called to mind fading photographs of factories and mills, smoking chimneys heaving under leaden skies, while grey, undernourished figures scurried or lounged about without purpose.

I had arranged digs, sight unseen, in a crumbling Victorian terraced house in Werneth Hall Road. They were the very opposite of the theatrical digs of comic legend and were run by a ruddy faced Irish washerwoman who organised the place like an army barracks. In some ways, I suppose, this was quite appropriate since, for me, this was National Service and the Varsity life rolled in one. She showed me to a room containing six mattresses littered about the floor. A selection of tatty singlets and moth eaten jerseys was piled on top of each. She pointed to one of the mattresses and with the dual injunction to 'take her as I found her' and 'expect nowt fancy 'ere', I was assigned my 'bed'. I was prepared to accept these broadbased rules of the house but two questions persisted. Who on earth were the five other occupants of this seedy place? And where were they? I was vaguely troubled by my father's story of the boots he feared would be stolen in the hostels he had frequented. But here there was not even a bedstead to stand in them. In spite of that, I settled down to an early night to face whatever the first day at the theatre would bring.

After a couple of hours sleep I was jolted awake by the loud arrival of a boozy, sweaty, arguing gang of men who barged past me to take possession each of his mattress. They took no notice of me but carried on coughing and smoking and exchanging their raucous banter. The room slowly filled with a tangible fog of sweat and smoke and beer as they, too, settled down to noisy sleep. I lay there not daring to speak and genuinely afraid of attack. Who they were remained a mystery, because when I awoke they had vanished as unexpectedly as they had arrived. I might have been tempted to think the episode had been part of an anxious dream, had it not been for the stale smell which hung over the room like soiled linen. With some relief I noticed that my shoes were still there.

I arrived at Oldham Rep. at nine sharp as the actors and stage crew were casually filing in. I liked them immediately. All of them greeted this shy, nervous lad from Liverpool, with warmth and concern – from the bluff character actors to the moody, introspective juvenile leads, from the alluring actresses to the effeminate limp-wristed old timers; this last category constituting a phenomenon at the time completely unknown to me. I knew, in that moment, my gamble was going to pay off. It all seemed so delightfully casual and disorganised and I instinctively felt at home. I spared a thought for the drudges stranded on the pierhead among the ships' manifests at the Dock Board and I thanked God I was here with this colourful, cheerful troupe.

The work felt right but everything else was depressingly wrong. At nights I was desperately homesick and alone. I cried myself to sleep regularly and took to reciting the Creed to try to console myself. It would have been easy to end the homesickness at a stroke of course, by going back to Liverpool, but I felt such an action would be a form of betrayal. I was not prepared to give my father the satisfaction of being proved right, that this disastrous little scheme was destined to be a passing fancy and I would be faced, like everybody else, to get a proper job. After all, had I not defended my intention so firmly at home? The shame and humiliation of a premature return would be too much for my stubborn nature to bear. So I was prepared to go through the agony of loneliness in the expectation that it would turn out right in the end. I lied to my parents in letters when I told them I had pleasant digs and was feeling fine. They asked to come over and see me once but I invented an excuse so that they were prevented from seeing what conditions I really lived in. In my worse moments I feared this was going to be some terrible replay of Dad's life in the doss houses, so I had to keep them away at all costs. But things improved.

By this time I had been introduced to my fellow ASM, an attractive girl called Enyd Williams, who instructed me in our allotted tasks, the first of which, each morning, was to make coffee for the cast before rehearsal. Oldham was weekly rep. then, so Tuesdays always began with a read through of the following week's play and a preliminary walk through the first act so that actors knew roughly where they could expect the furniture to be. It was a basic diet of middle brow drama, the odd Willis Hall, perhaps a bit of Shakespeare to raise the tone, an Agatha Christie and a panto at Christmas. As the cast rehearsed, Enyd and I sat in the wings making notes of the various props and dressings we would need and wondering how best to come by them. When they broke for lunch we would leave the theatre to beg or borrow whatever was needed – old fashioned gramophones, potted aspidistras, suits of armour, stuffed parrots, anything. More rehearsal followed in the afternoons, after which the ASMs would dress the set for the evening show, run the production from the wings and be let off home gone half past ten. The routine recurred seven days a week and was a gruelling exercise for us all. I never remember having time to sit down to a meal there. We survived on an endless supply of snacks – hot pork pies from the UCP (United Cowheel Products which were a feature of Northern towns of the day) and cheese sandwiches, which we ate on the job. Occasionally one of the actors would sneak us in half a shandy from the pub nearby to round off the meal. I was beginning to enjoy the life and feel at ease.

After the first few weeks of sleeping on the floor with the boozing navvies, I moved digs and any residual homesickness vanished. I was gradually befriended by a wonderful couple called Ted and Cath Blunt who let me have a room in their two up, two down terraced house opposite the stage door. He was the theatre caretaker and used to introduce himself by saying, 'I'm Ted Blunt. Blunt by name and blunt by bloody nature!' The two of them resembled a pair of caricatures on a Lancashire seaside postcard – Ted, gaunt and wiry, and Cath, big and loud, a warm earth mother who took me to her ample bosom. They looked after me and gave me a stable base, a second home. It was here that my parents came to see me, my father as bewildered as ever as to why I should continue with this faintly disreputable lifestyle. By this time, though, he could see that I was happy and well installed in my chosen career, so he was, however reluctantly, gradually resigning himself to the fact that his son was intent on this rather strange craft after all.

Cath Blunt seemed to spend her days brewing or, as she put it, 'mashing' tea, and chain smoking Park Drive. Their little house had no inside lavatory so on winter nights, when the biting gale came roaring down the street from the moors, answering the call of nature was a painful experience. Tiptoeing through the backyard in snow, ice and rain at three in the morning was a uniquely awful feature of life in those days so I decided it had to be curtailed. I borrowed a chamber pot from props to relieve myself in the comfort of my own room. I remember Bernard Miles recalling his days in theatrical digs and the landlady who, foreseeing this nocturnal practice, had pinned a notice in every room: 'Do not put chamber pots underneath the bed', it ran, 'as the steam will rust the springs'. There was no fear of that in the Blunt household, the room was so cold that any filament of warmth faded in a matter of moments. I would lie in bed watching my breath billowing above me. Relieving myself in the room was hardly more comfortable than outside. Inevitably the night came when relief was impossible as the pot was full. Taking it stealthily to the window I poured it down into the street below. In the course of this slovenly operation much of the liquid had adhered to the wall, leaving a telltale ice flow the length of the building. 'Bloody 'ell,' said Ted in the morning, 'that's ice up there. Where did that bloody lot come from?' I had not the nerve to enlighten him and hoped instead for an early thaw.

There was more drama at Oldham backstage than there ever seemed to be out front. One of the leading men at the time was Robert Keegan, who later played a prominent part in the long running TV series 'Z Cars'. One night I came within a whisker of murdering him. I suppose murder might have been overstating it. A plea of diminished responsibility or sudden madness may just have been acceptable in mitigation.

We were doing the Brian Rix farce, 'Reluctant Heroes', and as ASM I was responsible for lightning flashes, explosions and rattling the metal thunder sheet. The technology behind all this was a closed book to me but, rather than ask, I went ahead in semi-ignorance installing incendiary devices and explosive charges in the flies above the stage. Testing them all beforehand

[73]

was a luxury I judged we could not afford so the opening night was the only opportunity for the first run. The first night duly came and I waited for the appropriate cue from Robert Keegan centre stage. Nothing seemed to happen for a split second, then the most enormous multiple report shook the theatre. Smoke filled the auditorium and bits of debris and masonry began to bombard Mr Keegan who, at this time, was still centre stage. He stepped back a few paces and, as a culmination to this impromptu firework display, the great thunder sheet hurtled down, missing Keegan by inches and embedding itself in the floor. This rerun of the Blitz received a cheering ovation from the crowd and the curtain fell to great acclaim. I felt rather pleased it had all gone off reasonably well for a first attempt and could not understand why Keegan was so angry.

He was also involved in another curious incident in a production of Julius Caesar. At the point in the plot where Caesar, played by Keegan, is murdered, the text requires him to be taken off on a bier. Neither Enyd nor I knew what a bier looked like so we were forced to improvise. We deduced it must be something like a large wooden stretcher and would have to be constructed to bear the not inconsiderable weight of the Keegan frame. We decided that only something the size and strength of a door would do the trick and tracked down a pretty stout example back stage. On to this I nailed a sheet of hardboard, so that Keegan could meet his maker in comfort, and attached handles at either end.

It was at this stage that I made the crucial mistake which was to prove the leading man's undoing. I had nailed the hardboard shiny side up. At the dress rehearsal all went well until Caesar's dead body was placed reverently on the door. The minions then ran up to take the corpse away. Sadly the first minion arrived in position a second or two earlier than his colleague. As he lifted his end the bier tilted upwards and Julius Caesar, with no grip on the shiny hardboard, began to slide down the ramp. As the corpse could not be seen to come alive to arrest this unstoppable motion, the luckless cadaver could do nothing but slide off the stage into the orchestra pit like a half-hearted burial at sea. Again Mr Keegan failed to see the funny side of things and suspected I was mounting a personal vendetta against him.

After a short time at the theatre I began to get walk-on parts. Not very grand, to be sure, the third English nobleman for example or a major component of Burnham Wood in 'Macbeth', but at least I was up there on the stage creating a niche for myself as a useful little 'rude mechanical'. All the time I was learning new things. I was benefiting from being with people who spoke the Queen's English impeccably and I used them all as my models and teachers. I was gaining in confidence, learning how to mix with people of all different backgrounds and, most of all, the quality of my voice was developing. I was practising how to use it as an instrument rather than as a tool, how to project it to reach the back of the house, how to introduce moods of light and shade, how to pace my delivery, in short, how to speak well.

An added bonus was that you got to hold girls close to you without any danger of the police being called. One week I landed a plum part as the son of the house in a long forgotten domestic comedy. I was to play opposite the rather demure Audrey Muir-Mathesson, a prim and bossy girl at the time, who, I felt, rather disapproved of my uncouth Liverpool manner. In this flimsy piece of flummery I was supposed to be playing the part of a moustachioed young blood making desperate and pathetic attempts to seduce Miss Muir-Mathesson. The week's run had gone well and all that could have gone wrong, strangely enough, did not. Not until one Saturday evening performance, that is, when the tickets were sold out. A matinée had overrun and I was forced to change quickly. As a result I did not have time to glue on my moustache securely enough so, as a panic measure, I pencilled on a natty Italian job with a stick of eye-liner which was lying about in the dressing room. As I took a last glance in the mirror before going on stage I reckoned this was in fact much more effective than the strip of whisker I had been using until then.

The middle of Act One saw Miss Muir-Mathesson and me in a fiery clinch on the sofa, centre stage. I overdid the romantic acting with much heaving of the body and profound, lovelorn sighs. A moment later we were disturbed by a third party and Miss Muir-Mathesson rushed stage left to recover her composure. The drawback of my last minute make-up now became apparent to everyone but her as the audience saw the perfect imprint of my Neapolitan moustache on the pale top lip of the lovely Miss Muir-Mathesson. The image drew unexpected laughter from the audience, all the more exquisite for the look of blank incomprehension on the part of the leading lady. She, like Robert Keegan, sensed a nitwit at work.

Why they kept me on was a mystery to me, but they did, and I used the time to pick up everything I could. There was little social life as such outside the theatre, but a strong sense of team spirit within it. Working hours from nine until eleven meant you rarely met 'ordinary' people. Your life became your work and your work revolved round theatre people. I loved them and felt very much among friends who became as close as family. I felt like a grateful Nicholas Nickleby taken up by Vincent Crummles and accepted as one of the troupe. Tolerance was their over-riding quality, a complete lack of prejudice which showed itself in the way they took perfect strangers like me to their hearts. Their irreverent attitude to authority (and to Income Tax) and their acceptance of the human race, with all its foibles and in all its diversity were, for me, models of civilized behaviour and I was proud to be associated with them. I would look at people coming out of the mills and perhaps preparing to get dressed up for a night out and feel honoured that I would be doing the show that they would be paying money to see.

Sunday afternoon was the only free time we had to ourselves but despite the dog-tiredness I was happy and, for the moment, wanted nothing else. There was a lot still to be learnt before I launched myself in the BBC. The first thing was how not to upset a star actress who was visiting the theatre for a short run.

The star in question was the legendary Jessie Matthews, who had agreed to appear in one of our productions. The name of the play has long since escaped me but one aspect I shall never forget was the requirement for a white grand piano to figure prominently on stage.

I toured all the big stores of Oldham and Manchester pleading with unsympathetic managers to be loaned a grand piano for a week, in exchange for a tiny, meaningless credit in the programme. No-one was tempted by this generous offer so I had to change my strategy and took to combing second hand furniture shops where I eventually found the shell of an old concert grand complete with three rickety legs. After I had tidied it up, sanded it down and painted it, I thought, this would be ideal.

After a morning of home carpentry I managed to get this three legged monster to stand, unaided, centre stage. It was by now Sunday afternoon and the show opened the next day. As yet, though, the piano was still black and had to be painted white. I laid on a couple of coats of gloss paint as liberally as I could but, by six o'clock that evening, its colour had changed only to a muddy grey.

I returned at seven-thirty to see how well an extra coat had taken but was disappointed to notice little improvement. I lashed on more gloss paint for the next couple of hours but the piano refused to shine any whiter than a battleship grey. There were still a few hours before the show's opening so I worked through the night building up layer upon layer of white gloss until the piano would gleam and sparkle like something from a Hollywood musical.

By Monday morning the paint was less grey, to be sure, but had the disadvantage now of being glutinous to the touch. During the rest of the day I used a hair dryer to harden the paint which I then overlayed with more helpings of gloss to ensure that, by curtain up, to a short sighted pianist playing by low candlelight, the object before him would resemble a white grand piano.

At some point in the second act Miss Matthews was required to lean casually on the piano and break into song. My first prayer was answered. Namely that the three elderly legs would not wobble sideways and deposit our elegant chanteuse unceremoniously on the floor. But my second remained unheard. The hairdryer had proved inefficient. When the song came to an end Miss Matthews remained motionless. She had realised that the heat of her forearm, spread sensuously over the piano top, had melted the flimsy surface of the paint forcing the arm down into a half inch layer of wet Dulux. Her ballgown, too, had stuck to the side of the piano, making a stylish sweep downstage to take the applause impossible. As she prized herself off the sticky surface, traces of white paint were seen adhering to her hands and arms, and, most disastrously, to her long black ball gown.

I spent another sleepless night with the hairdryer after the performance had ended, but succeeded only in bringing the surface of the piano out in a series of ugly blisters. Throughout the remainder of the week Miss Matthews and the rest of the cast avoided all contact with the piano which, like some malevolent white whale removed from its element and mysteriously beached on stage, exuded a feeling of menace. By the end of the week the paint was still wet. And Jessie Matthews, for reasons best known to herself, never played Oldham again.

[78]

It was here that I got my first break in films when one morning a casting director, flamboyant in cloak and fedora, turned up at the stage door looking for character actors to feature in a film being made for the Billy Graham organization. The world famous evangelist, it seemed, was accompanying his legendary Christian crusades with an allegorical film depicting the change of heart and lifestyle that became possible if people turned to Christ. The film itself was to be a celluloid tract set in a typical working class Lancashire home and depicting, in transparently stereotyped form, a sullen, argumentative family much given to 'goin' down t'pub', 'livin' on t'tripe and cow'eel' and forever mashing tea. The plot was predictable enough. These surly individuals attend a Billy Graham rally one day and return home transformed into a happy and sweetnatured unit ready to spread the Word in their turn. The Fedora Hat cast Robert Keegan as the heavy father, a delightful character actress called Nellie Hanham as Mam, Enyd as the daughter, and me as the rebellious young son – a subnormal, Lancastrian James Dean in a Fair Isle woolly.

The location was a terraced house (every house within a radius of twelve miles was a terraced house) in Fallowfield. We were booked to spend ten days there. In comparison to the techniques of theatre the mechanics of film making were confusion itself. We shot the last scene first and then spent long periods nodding or scowling into the camera. Everything, down to the smallest reaction shot, needed doing a dozen times, at the end of which constant repetition had rendered the lines meaningless to the point that we forgot them. The second location for this turgid drama was the New Theatre Bar in the centre of Manchester – a watering hole which offered some relief to the members of the crew and cast. After the pub had closed one Saturday night we all moved in, accompanied by mountains of equipment, to spend all the hours of darkness filming a scene which, when projected on screen, was to last a full thirty seconds. But even this scene was rehearsed and re-shot countless times before the director judged we had a take. We were playing a vaguely dissolute family out on the tiles and, on location at the New Theatre Bar, life began to imitate art as benevolent well-wishers plied us with an endless supply of drinks the whole night through. When filming ended at dawn we staggered out onto the streets as if just despatched from some Bacchanalian orgy and vaguely wondering why the shooting had taken so long.

The finished product was called 'A Touch of Brass', and was greeted with universal waves of indifference. Some months later I saw the picture as some sort of supporting B film. The audience refused to take it seriously and, whether oblivious to, or contemptuous of, the implicit spiritual message, treated the whole show as a huge joke and whispered their own sceptical commentary as the drama unfolded. Under different circumstances I would have been tempted, in an exaggeratedly subtle way, to draw attention to myself as an up-and-coming film star but, sensing the mood of a critical public, I wisely kept quietly anonymous.

My film debut, however, did have one powerful advantage. It was lucrative. For the sort of money I had been offered, I mused, perhaps being laughed at wasn't such a bad experience after all. At the theatre I was being paid £4 15s for a 90 hour week. These Hollywood moguls were paying ten pounds a day. I began seriously to consider tax exile. I also began to feel it was time to move on.

In many ways the filming episode was the spur to action. I had been at Oldham Rep. for a year and, bearing in mind that acting was never to be a job in itself for me, merely the means to achieving my goal as BBC announcer, I judged it wise to leave for more experience. Where better to head for than

London, where professionals and public alike would take me to their heart in solemn respect for my wisdom, talent, and breadth of experience. I was twenty at the time, planning the second phase of my career as an ASM in some West End show where I would be in the thick of the real action.

I said my farewells to the cast, some of whom tried to persuade me to reconsider my rash decision and who warned me that getting on in the capital was trickier in reality than it seemed in expectation. I was unmoved. Ted and Cath were sad to see me go, as I was to leave them, but I was now clear in my mind that a change was needed if I were not to waste the precious and limited time I had to see my ambitions fulfilled. I was desperate to do everything I had to do by the age of twenty-five. After that it would be too late.

Mentally and financially I was buoyant, bobbing along on a calm sea in full sunshine – unaware at the time, however, that I had not yet left the harbour and that beyond the jetty choppier waters waited. With the £110 I had earned 'from films' I went to Manchester to buy three suits, ten shirts, four pairs of shoes, a pint of Robinsons bitter and twenty Players, and then, boarding the bus from the coach station on a warm spring evening of 1962, set off for the big time, where the doors of every theatrical agency in the city would be flung open in welcome.

[5]

I trudged down miles of seedy corridor, up thousands of well worn steps, and the doors of every theatrical agency in the city remained firmly shut.

London was a mean place, full of surly people who were not aware of my presence and, when they were, were resentful of it. I quickly found digs and, with an unerring nose for the bizarre, settled in to a madhouse behind Marble Arch, run by the St Dunstan's Organization. The landlord and his wife were welcoming and polite but somehow distant at the same time. Then I realised that not only were they both blind but they were blind drunk into the bargain. As they moved they dislodged gin bottles, collided with the cat and caused me to alternate between laughter and concern for their physical well being. At night there was no rest to be had, thanks to the interminable slamming of doors and their muttered curses as they staggered around vainly remembering where the lavatory was.

Throughout this time I never lost sight of my aim. Although I was in no position to take the citadel of broadcasting by storm I was able to reconnoitre the territory by day in disguise. Since no stage work was available I had got a temporary job in a tobacconist's shop in Regent Street just a few hundred yards away from Broadcasting House itself. At lunchtimes I used to walk in gingerly through the heavy doors into the grand entrance hall where I sat watching the comings and goings of the famous as if I had some important business to attend to with the likes of John Snagge and Stuart Hibberd. If I had felt at home in the theatre, I felt much more so here. A powerful sense of excitement was generated at the mere thought that the sound studios were a few yards away. I wanted to belong to this world, wanted my life to be connected with this glorious building and all it represented.

I lasted barely a week at the tobacconist's. Old St Jasper's Ready Rubbed Shag had a tenuous appeal which I was glad to renounce. What was problematical now, though, was how I should proceed professionally because with no money coming in from any source and no prospect of theatrical employment in London there was little reason to stay down south at all. The alternative, going home to face a smug I-told-you-so from my father, was, in the end, the humiliating lesser of two evils.

For an unfortunate two weeks I returned to Liverpool trying half-heartedly to sell office furniture. Terrified lest anybody agreed to buy one of the items on sale – the terror sprang from my ignorance of the invoice system – I spent all my time persuading customers to go away and think the matter over, by which time one of the other hapless floorwalkers might be on hand to clinch the deal.

In April 1962 I applied for the combined position of Assistant Stage Manager and juvenile lead with the Mercury Players in a summer season in Devon. The players performed at the Manor Pavilion in Sidmouth and would, I hoped, be anxious to recruit me to allow them to scale grand theatrical heights. The producer there was Ron Govey, who seemed impressed enough by my past record at Oldham to give me the job.

The great bonus of the Sidmouth engagement was that it was part of a finite run. I knew in advance that the job was destined to end in the autumn so I could take full advantage of the experience, learning all I had to learn, but in a relaxed sort of way. The University of Life is a cliché which was, despite its by now tired associations, accurate and apt to describe my theatrical

[83]

days before joining the BBC. It was my training period and, like the summer season in Sidmouth, marked out, in college-style terms, where I would add more to my expertise.

In those days a Liverpool accent was associated inescapably with comedians. To have the Scouse twang was to be seen as warm hearted, quick witted and good humoured but never to be taken seriously. My accent was improving but it was still not quite right if I wanted to get work on the radio where, outside comedy shows, a Northern or, for that matter, any other regional accent, was not countenanced. Sidmouth was about as far away as one could be from that Northern environment and meant that all the vocal influences on me would be good ones. I learnt just as assiduously as if I had been a university freshman, newly despatched to a venerable place of study. And I had a memorably carefree time.

Oldham may have had a proper theatre but it was grim and grey in comparison with Sidmouth. Life here was a perpetual holiday and made up in full measure for the one serious professional drawback; that it did not have a theatre – or not one to speak of. The Manor Pavilion was no bigger than a church hall with loose chairs arranged in rows, the sort of place which might play host to returning missionaries and their explanatory slide shows, but which could surely not be expected to double up as a legitimate theatre by night. But it was here, on a stage the size of a large kitchen table, that we were expected to perform theatrical miracles in front of a holiday audience intent on live entertainment. Occasionally our efforts, ill rehearsed and fantastically under-resourced, would provoke unexpected giggles or derisory laughter, but at least it was a reaction and to be preferred to the menacing silence which would sometimes greet our dramatic presentations.

It was a small company – it was a small theatre – comprising seven actors of whom my colleague, Arthur, and I were expected to be, in addition, stage managers, carpenters, electricians, set designers and decorators. The season was about twelve weeks long with two shows a week. We would open for the Thursday matinée and run until the following Wednesday night when the set would be struck and a new play would be launched. The philosophy behind this odd schedule was that those booked in for a week's holiday, which was invariably from Saturday to Saturday, would be able, should they desire further punishment, to come to the theatre twice. No Shakespeare here, of course. Agatha Christie, Victorian melodrama, and frothy farces were the preferred diet.

The most difficult and tiring part of the schedule was the midweek changeover. After the Wednesday evening perform-ance we would work all night taking down the old set and installing the new one, decorating it and laying out the props in readiness for the new show on Thursday afternoon.

Many a week we got so behind with our work that often the curtain would go up on a set which the actors were only then seeing for the first time. Quite often, as a result of some overnight technical hitch, windows and doors would be transposed and the hearth would be where the hat stand should have been. This led to the curious spectacle of vicars striding in boldly through the fireplace and policemen clambering in awkwardly through the sash window. On one memorable occasion Hercule Poirot tossed his hat casually on the fire.

What the Sidmouth audiences made of all this is not recorded; they still continued to fill most of the wooden seats and the odd notice in the local paper reported minor successes, alongside our minor disasters. The actors put up with conditions with great stoicism but occasionally the nervous strain would begin to tell. One of the members of the company was a woman called Frances Lovering who, in her younger days, had been the toast of the West End, but who was now somewhat reduced and relied on this kind of tenuous summer season to eke out a precarious living. She was also beginning to have trouble remembering her lines. In one of the productions that summer Frances had to stand alone, centre stage, to deliver a lengthy monologue of some three or four pages in duration.

I was in the prompt book in the wings one evening when she began her soliloquy in fine declamatory style. After a line or two she began to falter and I threw in the odd word to help her. The speech degenerated rather quickly after that, until I was eventually speaking more and more of her lines than she was. The audience looked at her immobile face on stage while listening to some deep male voice from the wings and stared on in blank disbelief as though they were watching a peculiarly innovative form of ventriloquism.

In the end Frances became so distressed that she fled from the stage in tears. So as not to render the plot utterly incomprehensible I felt I ought to carry on from the wings. The audience sat there agape, as all the while my disembodied voice intoned the lines meant for a, by now invisible, actress on an empty stage. In some quarters it was greeted as an astonishing piece of avant-garde theatre.

More disasters lay ahead, one of them confirming the great theatrical truth that stage guns work only when they are not intended to. In a forgettable production of 'Johnny Belinda' I played a gun-toting madman who was supposed to shoot the girl as she lay cowering behind one of the bales of hay in the far corner. The actual sound of the gunshot would come from a blank that Arthur would fire off stage. At the crucial moment I aimed the gun and pulled the trigger. Nothing. The girl continued to cower and I continued to click. Click, click, silence. The plot demanded her death in this scene, or the story would make no sense, so I quickly thought of another way to despatch her.

[86]

I remembered the knife that hung from my belt and began to draw it menacingly but the knife was snarled up in the sheath and, try as I might, it would not come loose. In a blind panic I left the knife, flung the gun aside, moved purposefully towards the girl, hoping to pounce on her and attempt strangulation. Half way across the stage Arthur's gun finally went off, taking killer and victim by surprise. The girl had the presence of mind to fall over and by now the audience, clearly baffled as to the immediate cause of death, was at least convinced she was quite seriously deceased. Not even Johnny Belinda's victim could have survived shots from two different guns, an attempted stabbing and intended throttling. I snarled melodramatically to cover the illogicality of the scene but the audience remained puzzled.

Northern, working-class dramas were very much in vogue at the time and we thought it only right to inflict one on the good people of Sidmouth by way of awakening them to the gritty realities of life outside the cosy south. In fact they were so popular, spawning the likes of Albert Finney and Tom Courtenay and a whole new wave of regional talent, that for a time I questioned the wisdom of losing my Scouse accent. Not that it would have served me well in the particular production we had planned, since I was consigned to back-stage operations – not so much 'Room at the Top' as 'Stuck at the Bottom'.

The set called for a working gas cooker and real kitchen sink up stage. Rigging up the cooker was no problem but the sink was a bit of a poser. The only water supply was the fire hose which threatened to provide too powerful a jet for the few drops of water we needed to fill the kettle. But the fire hose seemed the only way.

I bought two lengths of tubing and fixed them to the taps, then ran the tubing along to the main hose, whose diameter was unfortunately several times bigger than the rubber tube. By poking the smaller inside the larger, filling up the gap with rags and then swathing the whole joint in several hundred yards of insulating tape I managed to produce a healthy dribble of water from the taps on stage.

At the beginning of Thursday's opening performance all seemed to be going well; kettles were being filled and gas cookers puttering away nicely. But out of sight of the audience my makeshift joint was coming under increasing strain and evidence of this development was becoming clear on stage as a dark stain began to appear beneath the sink. The stain, glistening now under the lights, began to spread slowly down the carpet towards the sofa where the leading actors sat and, as the act wore on, the damp transferred itself to their socks. They were beginning to wonder why there was a curious sloshing noise every time they moved when I, rather belatedly, decided it was time to switch off the hose. By now, of course, the water was everywhere and the gritty Northern drama seemed to be set in a creeping Louisiana swamp.

Sidmouth was great fun, a careless interlude signifying nothing. We worked all hours but found time enough to get drunk on rough cider. We slept on the beach, bathed in the nude and all summer long had no plans for tomorrow. The Mercury Players seemed to have a fair proportion of homosexual actors among them and, not being myself that way inclined, I found to my surprise and delight, that I was rather in demand among female company. For a young lad of twenty it was very flattering to be the centre of attention when there were so many pretty actresses around. I suppose I went a bit mad and put the serious study of my craft on hold for the time being. I was convinced, however, that none of this rich experience would be wasted, that I could, much later on, draw on it with profit. It was confirmation, if I really needed it, that the nine to five life was not to be for me. I enjoyed the chaotic conditions and the feeling that I was

[88]

working when everybody else was playing. Going against the grain has always had a charm for me.

The season was nearing its end now and two productions remained. The first had been an earlier triumph of ours, a Bertie Wooster farce, which we decided to take on a tour of Beer, Seaton and Lyme Regis. We encountered predictable problems struggling to shoehorn our travelling set into the variety of small-scale venues we played at. When there was no space for a window we left it out and actors would stare at a blank wall and pronounce the weather nice for the time of year. As a result of a late substitution of French windows for the fireplace, the ever resourceful Jeeves was seen heaving a bucket of coal on to the garden terrace. Nobody seemed to mind, nor, for that matter, care.

In the last week of the run the company was joined by Alan Lake, a strange Romany boy with a haunted look, who later married Diana Dors. What attracted him to Lyme Regis we never discovered but he was there when I made my theatrical farewell, engineering the downfall of 'Salad Days'.

By our standards this was a complicated show with a complicated lighting plot, calling for more changes than I had been used to. Our dimmer boards – the technical equipment that allowed us to fade the lighting up and down – were not designed to take the increased load we were putting on it and on the opening night it crackled and fizzed alarmingly. As a precaution I even took to fading up the switches with a wooden stick to avoid electrocution. The system lasted to within minutes of the final curtain when the strain became too much. Blue flashes were followed by a loud explosion and the theatre settled into a troubled darkness.

The summer season had ended with a bang and ushered out those easy days playing skittles in the pubs and the languid nights lying with pretty girls in the long grass by the River Sid.

It was sad to leave, but the theatrical life was taking on a predictability of which I was beginning to grow faintly weary. I had tried my hand at auditions for the BBC during this time, and even tried my luck with the regional TV station, but had had no success. It was the chicken-and-egg type of situation with which anyone who has considered a job in broadcasting will be entirely familiar. I could not get the job because I had no broadcasting experience and I could not hope to get that experience until I had landed the job.

The only answer lay, for the time being, in more theatre. I answered an advert in 'The Stage' for a juvenile lead in a six month season at Swansea Rep. which I judged would be, at least, a cosy home for the winter and would give me time to marshal my forces for a full-scale attack on the radio. My chief memory of the time is not a theatrical one at all but a gastronomic one of daunting proportions.

My landlady in Swansea was a Mrs Alice Jones who lived in a cluttered little house in Beech Street. She prided herself on keeping a good table and expected her guests to do it justice. Sundays started with a breakfast of cornflakes, porridge, fried eggs, potatoes, bacon, tomatoes, mushrooms, sausages and occasionally a slab of liver. There was fried bread, too, toast, marmalade and generous servings of strong tea from an industrial urn. Barely had I recovered from the blow-out when elevenses – tea and home-made biscuits – would appear. Lunch, an hour later, incorporated meat, veg, and potatoes by the ton. I was warned to be back by 4 sharp when tea would be served from a trolley of cake, scones, strawberry jam, bread, butter and cling peaches. I think Mrs Jones realised she had overloaded the system and when my stomach gave an ominous heave I was permitted to retire defeated to bed.

My engagement in Swansea was due to last six months – that much work I had been promised by the particularly charming director who had hired me. He even hinted that more work might later become available for the right boy. The precise qualification for the job became clear within the first few days of my arrival at the theatre. The director was becoming rather too fond of his protégé than his protégé wished. In short he was taking a shine to me in a way I could not accept, still less reciprocate. The more I resisted his advances the more forceful he became until a definite aggression made the situation unbearable. I could have shown the good Christian virtue of turning the other cheek but under the circumstances that could have been worse. I left.

Technically I was fired and decided once more to return to Liverpool where my Dad, warned in advance by letter, viewed the whole episode as yet one more ignominious chapter in my life history. For him it was not so much a temporary setback as full and final proof that I was barking up the wrong tree. Larking about in this limp-wristed world, he said, was bound to lead to all this upset.

He was wrong of course, simply because he did not understand me or the generous people with whom I had been privileged to spend almost two years of my life. The theatre had given me much. Its lovely people had taught me a lot and provided me with the training and the preparation I needed. I salute and embrace those men and women with whom I shared those formative years and thank them without reserve for their help, their support and their love. When I left Swansea my theatrical days were over for good.

It was a sad journey from Wales to Liverpool. I reflected on all that had passed, viewed the uncertainty of the future with alarm and rehearsed a plausible excuse I could present to my father to save face. I was mulling over Mark IV of this excuse when the train I had boarded clanked its way into Exchange Station in Manchester, where I had to change. It was a murky

November afternoon and as we slowly neared our destination we passed the Granada building. For one so despondent as me the building seemed to exude an enviable confidence as it shone like a beacon across the waste ground to the railway embankment. The red neon sign – GRANADA TV NETWORK – seemed such an optimistic anomaly in this disconsolate skyline that I felt immediately cheered. 'There must be more to broadcasting than the BBC', I thought, 'Granada must employ announcers and newsreaders. Why not give it a try?'

There and then I interrupted my journey, headed for the studio building and asked to see the man who was in charge of the announcers. His name was Norman Frisby, a charming man with an easy going personality who happened also to be from Liverpool. He asked me what I had done and what experience of broadcasting I had had, to which the answer was acutely embarrassing. I had tales enough of theatrical work and walk-on parts but a hopeless depression came over me when I was forced to admit I had never set foot inside radio or television studios and had never handled a microphone professionally. It occurred to me that I ought to have caught the first railway connection home instead of calling up such self imposed agony and humiliation.

But Norman was kind and left me some hope that all was not lost. He took my home address and promised to get in touch if anything came up. Even with my limited experience I knew that this was a euphemism for, 'Thank you very much and goodbye.' But Norman was a genuine guy and meant what he said.

Afterwards I hung around in the main reception area and watched. From time to time one of the stars of 'Coronation Street', only two years old then, would flit through, and I recall thinking that OK, this wasn't Broadcasting House but it was broadcasting and, if I were to be offered a job on the spot, yes, I might seriously consider it. I was not offered anything there and then and felt, unreasonably, rather angry as a result. I returned to Liverpool by the next available train, tolerated my father's sarcastic asides and settled into the by now familiar routine of scouring 'The Stage' for opportunities and for jobs which, if I had been honest with myself, I had to admit I no longer really enjoyed.

Ten days later I received a telegram at home. POSSIBILITY RELIEF ANNOUNCER DUTY NEXT WEEK. RING NORMAN FRISBY, GRANADA. SOONEST.

[6]

If broadcasting was my vocation then these eleven stark words
on a telegram sent to a small house in Waterloo constituted the
call. Telegrams were unknown things in our household, as they
were for everyone else we knew, and their arrival, when they
were handed over in person by the postman, signified the worst.
They could mean only sickness or death. They might just have
been welcomed as confirmation that the lucky recipient had won
£75,000 on the pools but, by and large, they were feared. When
the news came through, hand delivered to me in person, it was
even more seductive than any jackpot or windfall could be.

I told Mum and Dad, and even my Dad was moved grudgingly
to admit I might, after all, be getting somewhere. Although we
did not have a television at the time, he knew that Granada was
a big organisation and what it specialised in was legitimate.
None of the grease paint and fancy dress. He even offered me
a few words of encouragement and chipped in to buy me a
new suit. Impressing your employer was something he could
understand. This was territory with which he was at last familiar.

We agreed that I would present myself at the Granada building
on the following Monday where Norman Frisby was waiting for
me. He told me that one of the announcers had gone sick and
that there was a vacancy for a replacement in a day or so. Then
he showed me round. Now, at last, I was on the inside of the
business not an anonymous onlooker full of unsatisfied longings
and expectation.

He showed me into what was known as the continuity suite.

This was really the centre of operations. Individual programmes were made in separate studios around the building but were linked by the announcer from the continuity suite. Programmes might be recorded and feature films broadcast but the one linking phenomenon was the continuity announcer and all his work was live. If a programme ran longer than it should (or, worse still, less than it was meant to) he would have to fill in effortlessly and casually to disguise any hitches in transmission so that the viewer was confident of watching a seamless evening's television. And, as all the various programmes in some way came to a point in the continuity studio, the announcers were responsible for giving the ensemble a feeling of unity. Stamping something of their character on it without distracting an audience; giving, in short, the multiplicity of shows, plays, films, serials, a Granada identity.

Standing in a studio that very first time was a thrill and there was no hiding it. Funnily enough the set-up seemed quite familiar. Although I had never seen microphones suspended in front of television monitors before, with faders to control the lot, it all seemed perfectly natural and undaunting. Perhaps it was the brashness of youth or, perhaps again, it was just that in some way I was destined for all this so there was no need to feel fear in the face of something preordained.

The continuity script from the night before lay on the desk and I idly thumbed through it. In those days Granada transmissions used to close down for a couple of hours in the afternoon and we were just approaching the time when the announcer would signal the break before transmission of the legendary test card. Without warning Frisby said, 'Would you like to try yourself out on air?' There was a slight pause during which feelings and thoughts collided in my head. Surely it can't be as simple as this, I thought, surely this thing I've waited for all my life can't really be done so unceremoniously.

And, anyway, how come this guy is prepared to trust such a beginner with this awesome responsibility. 'Yes please', I said.

I sat down, cleared my throat and waited for the red light before opening the microphone and saying, 'Granada Television is now closing down for the afternoon. We do hope you will join us again for our evening's entertainment which starts with children's programmes at five o'clock. So, for the moment, goodbye.' I was quivering with excitement like a little boy who has just learnt to ride a two wheeled bike. Frisby seemed quite pleased with my performance and had no idea that the thrill of doing what for him was a perfectly ordinary task was an experience more exciting than anything I could ever have imagined, and one I longed to repeat at the earliest possible moment.

Frisby suggested I might like to stay and open up the evening's transmission, an offer which I instantly accepted, not believing my good fortune. I delivered that first announcement of the evening with a similar potent thrill. I loved the ambience of the whole thing, the tension of the red light, the timing, the rehearsal of the script, the discipline of having to get it right first time with no chance of a retake, and, most of all, the feeling of intimacy with millions of fireside viewers in the North of England. I loved to give the phrase, 'From the North, this is Granada', a particular flourish. It was a disappointing moment when the evening announcer took over at half past six and I was forced to drag myself away. Like an excited schoolboy (and in fact I wasn't much past that stage) I considered this the best day of my life, capped by Frisby saying, as I left, 'Would you like to come back tomorrow?'

There seemed to be two main announcers at the time. One was an urbane fellow called Norman Somers, who sported suede shoes and a velvet jacket. He seemed to ooze an easy sophistication and had the habit of sleeping soundly with his feet on the desk during the long lull in the afternoons. The other,

Shortly after arriving in the Metropolis

Outside broadcast, 1974

With Kenny Ball on a live radio outside broadcast in Colchester. On the right, Steve Allen

Above: In the South of France with Alma, 1973.
Left: With Johnnie Mathis, 1975

Above: Looking out at Broadcasting House, Langham Place from St George's Hotel. *Below*: Blackheath with Greenwich in the background

Above: Radio outside broadcast in downtown Deptford, 1985. *Below*: Ken Griffin, Tim Rice, Angela Rippon, Liz Griffin and myself

Surrounded by the paraphernalia of broadcasting

Left to right: Chris Morgan, Michael Ford, Bob Holness, Bruce Wyndham, Cyril Drake, Ian Fenner, Bernard Manning, Ray Moore, Paul Hollingdale, Louisa Jane White

At Shepherds Bush, 1987, with Ken Bruce, Terry Wogan, Derek Jameson, and Colin Berry

With Terry Wogan at a Variety Club Award

Alma and I with Alan Freeman

Above: With Perry Como at a Record Reception at the Café Royal. *Left*: Ken Bruce and Alma at Gleneagles, 1983

The merry trio—Ken Bruce, myself and Jimmy Young

Champagne with Tom Jones

Left: Alma and I set off for the
London to Brighton race.
Below: Terry Waite and I
switch on Blackheath
Christmas lights

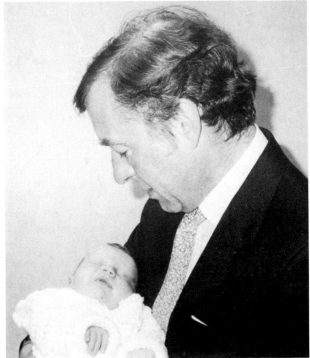

Above: David's
wedding day,
Manchester, 1980.
Right: Alma's first
grandchild in my
arms, May 1987

Left: Rolf Harris supports us on the bog-eyed jog. *Below*: Graham Lambourne and Dennis O'Keeffe. In Edinburgh on the bog-eyed jog

Max Boyce supports us too

Chatting to Mike Berry at 7.00 a.m. in Portsmouth

Dennis and I after a live outside broadcast. Dennis, as usual, is larking about. I am concentrating on an in-depth interview on a posy-phone with one of the local radio stations

in complete contrast, was Bernard Youens, later to become Coronation Street's Stan Ogden. He was an irascible man in his forties with, let us say, a rather full figure. He would come flapping up the corridor in his blue gaberdine mac, huffing and puffing and in a permanent sweat.

Bernard had been an actor who had served his time at the Rusholme Empress, the Ardwick Empire and other outposts of Northern culture. He had learnt his trade thoroughly but, unlike me, had stuck to it for rather longer. In the late 1950's he began picking up the odd television part, and when 'Coronation Street' was booked for an initial six week run, Bernard was offered the part of the landlord of the Rover's Return. At the time, with the chronic insecurity that only actors will ever know, he turned it down in preference to the security of a staff announcer's job. Money was a perpetual worry to him as it is to many in that risky and honourable profession.

Like a lot of old actors, Bernard had often dreamed of giving up his life on the road and settling down into a stable life for once. For him that dream meant calling a halt to his constant moves from theatre to theatre and digging himself into the cosy snug of a little pub somewhere in the sticks. He could, when the mood took him, be amply suited to the life, a beaming publican dispensing mugs of foaming ale beneath oak beams and by a blazing log fire. Towards the end of the 50's he tried to turn this dream into a reality and, as so often happens, the fragility of those dreams was ill suited to the hard knocks it received. He and his family sank their savings into what sounded like a hopeless, old, broken down gin palace in Preston. The place did not seem to attract the locals and any passing trade simply passed. So much so that Bernard decided that the only way to keep the stock moving was to shift it himself and doubtless Bernard's stature owed something to the constant pressure on him to keep the brewers happy with his turnover.

The set up could not last and, after a while, his dream became his personal nightmare and his short association with the licensed victualling trade came to an ignominious end, surrounded as he now was by creditors and debts. A regular income had by this time become an urgent priority, so he took the staff job at Granada to feed the kids.

But even that was not enough to keep assorted wolves from the door so he took on an extra job delivering bread in the daytime. His training as an actor had taught him to be in all things resourceful and anyone who has worked in that world is well schooled in ingenuity to get by. Bernard would rise at the crack of dawn and be on the road all day. By late afternoon he would park his bread van out of sight, a few streets away from the Granada building, and come to the studio to do the evening shift. Frequently he could barely keep his eyes open.

The routine was punishment for Bernard but offered a real opportunity for me – and one from which both of us stood to benefit. I got experience and he got some shut-eye. When Bernard staggered in to relieve me, who had been on the air all day, I could then say, 'God, you look tired, Bunny. Why don't you go home? I'll carry on. I don't mind at all'. He would then toddle off for a couple of liveners at the Victoria and I would carry on in the studio until closedown. It was a form of voluntary, unpaid overtime for which I got nothing but experience and deep personal satisfaction. Nobody at Granada minded as long as the job was done. At the age of twenty I was the youngest announcer on the ITV network.

I still had no clear idea of how long this would all last but, on the Friday of that first week, Frisby asked me if I would like to come back next week. The very question was academic and, as the weekend dragged by, every moment away from the studio seemed wasted. This gloriously nonchalant arrangement eventually lasted two and a half years.

[98]

Looked at from the outside the job I was doing could seem rather slight and one which it is hard to see justifying the inordinate enthusiasm I felt. I have often tried to rationalise my feelings towards it and never with complete success. It defied rational analysis in the end because it amounted to an obsession. It owes a lot to a feeling of egocentricity, the notion of 'when I speak, millions listen'. As an actor, of course, I was communicating to an audience, but the theatre lacked a dimension which I needed – the formal discipline of it all perhaps. The radio and, for the time being at Granada, the television gave the spoken word a quiet authority which I felt was absent in the theatre and bestowed on the announcers a certain gravitas which I, Enyd, and Arthur could never hope to aspire to in the wings of the Oldham Rep. or the Manor Pavilion. Perhaps I was more like my father than I dared admit and shared his longing for the stable life with just a touch of the exotic to taste. But there was more to it than that. Certainly the BBC men were forever associated with the events they described and that, to my mind, lent them an enviable stature. At Granada I was still a very long way from acquiring that stature.

The routine in Manchester was offering the prospect of permanence now, so I decided to settle in the city and rented a flat in Lapwing Lane in Didsbury. The word 'flat' creates an unjustifiably grand impression because this was no more than a cubby hole under the roof of a large Victorian pile which housed dozens of other disparate characters. The garret contained a single bed, a sink, a gas cooker, a table and a wardrobe and, as I bent low to enter the room, the furniture looked like the contents of a dolls' house which I, Gulliver-like, had wandered into by accident. Merely trying to move from the bed to the door without falling over something was a taxing logistical exercise.

The whole house was divided up into rooms like this which were occupied by single, mostly older, men whom I never met and barely heard. The ground floor was occupied by two landladies in the Bette Davis mould, a slightly menacing pair of women, resembling sinister figures in a psychological thriller, who seemed to loom up round every corner at all hours of the day and night. Whatever the weather or the season they were invariably dressed in ancient cardigans and heavy duty tweed skirts. In fact there was something about their gnarled and faded features that made it seem that they had been hand-knitted themselves. They, and the house, had a brooding quality which was not altogether pleasant. In the night floorboards would creak loudly as though responding to the tread of passing feet on the landing.

It had all the charm of the Bates Motel but at least it was home and I was now living an independent life, with no worries of having to fit in with somebody else's routine. There was no sergeant major barking out orders, no itinerant navvies bedding down beside me, no outside lavatory promising a painful nocturnal jaunt, and no insistent hostess threatening to drive me to an early grave with Gargantuan breakfasts. It was mine . . . or very nearly so.

During a wonderfully torrid affair with a dark haired vixen who also worked at the studios, I remember suggesting we sneak back to my room one afternoon. By some miracle the sentries must have been changing guard and we slipped in unnoticed, creeping into my doll's house like naughty children. As the pair of us got down to the serious business of the afternoon I began to be aware of low muffled breathing from the landing behind the locked bedroom door. By this time we were both well beyond the point of no return and we concluded our business in what we thought was silence. The breathing from outside continued through the long afternoon but it suddenly stopped when it began to go dark and we got dressed ready to leave. Again, miraculously, neither of the old ladies was around and we stole away into the evening.

Later that night I returned to find a scrawled note poked under the door. 'Mr Moore', it ran, 'my sister and I have certain standards and we would be obliged if you would respect them. If not, we are sure there must be other accommodation more suited to your taste.' Nothing further was said about the incident and it was a discreet reminder that, though I might feel a man of the world with an independent lifestyle, I was still only twenty and, until I really made it big, I was still reduced to living in other peoples' houses. My Jezebel, meanwhile, said she rather enjoyed making love quietly and suggested we did it again.

These glorious days at Granada just got better and better. I imagined that the novelty of being on air would wear off after a couple of weeks but in fact the excitement increased. The flat in Lapwing Lane had its drawbacks but I was spending so little time there it did not matter at all. All my waking hours seemed to be spent in the studios.

Bernard Youens liked our one-sided working arrangement and we became good friends. Together we used to pop into favourite bars dotted around Quay Street: the New Theatre Bar, scene of my great cinematic moment, the Victoria frequented by actors on tour and one tiny ale house known by the name of the landlady, a Mrs Moore. She, a tiny dot, barely drawing level with the mahogany counter, peered birdlike over the bar and smiled as she pulled pints of Robinsons. We used to go in there from time to time with Peter Adamson, Coronation Street's Len Fairclough, and Bernard would regale me with his wonderful old theatrical tales of hair-raising productions he had taken part in, as a member of Harry Hanson's Court Players and the legendary Frank Fortesque Company. It was a matter of great professional pride that I could match a few of his stories with my own from Sidmouth and Oldham. I felt on a par with him despite the gap in age, and the experiences we shared corroborated the feeling I had always had: that nothing is wasted and all one's past can be brought into the service of the present to enrich one's life and give it meaning.

In the confines of Mrs Moore's tiny bar it was often impossible to sit down. Every available inch was being used – and not just for social drinking. Frequently Tony Warren, the creator of Coronation Street, could be seen furiously scribbling away on scraps of paper, surrounded by pint mugs, at next week's episode of The Street. On every other flat surface around him there seemed to be more sheets of text, the whole thing representing a marvellously casual way of creating one of television's most popular programmes.

The atmosphere at the time, both in the pubs and the studios, was that of a very large and contented family. Actors, journalists, announcers, producers, writers, secretaries, all mixed easily with no sense of demarcation. The company was young and so were the people working for it – or if they weren't they were young enough at heart to lend the enterprise a freshness and a cohesion that generated a great sense of belonging. And if Granada was a happy fraternity, then the presiding genius and embodiment of benevolent paternalism was Sydney Bernstein, the founder of this burgeoning empire. He was very much the shirt-sleeves boss, always around the studio, popping his head round the continuity suite to see that all was well and taking seriously our humdrum moans about the air conditioning and the canteen food.

On Friday nights he would often host dinner parties in his penthouse suite on the roof of the building and after closedown I would pass him in the foyer and then see him standing on the steps waving farewell to his guests. On occasions like these his tall, dignified frame would be clothed in full evening dress with tails. As he stood there silhouetted against the lights of the building that housed his creation he reminded me for all the world of Scott Fitzgerald's 'Last Tycoon'.

It was at Granada that I first met Parky, plain Michael Parkinson then. He was very helpful to me from the moment I joined. He himself, with his established track-record in journalism, was one of the main reporters on Scene at Six Thirty, the evening's regional news and current affairs programme. It was tremendously popular at the time with a blend of hard news and magazine features which pulled in the big tea-time audiences. I had admired Parkinson's writing greatly even though I was never too keen on sport, in which he specialised. What I liked was his wit, his style and his talent for finding the right word and phrase to capture a moment. He brought that talent to his on-screen reporting and was well established in the medium when I came. So to me he was a venerable figure with a lot of weight and presence. He could easily have played the big star to the impressionable young announcer but he never did. There were one or two who could come on rather grand with the big 'I am' approach, but he was never one of them. With great kindness and straight Yorkshire concern he gave me all the advice I needed.

I have not forgotten a small event which took place when Parkinson's fame was at its height. It was only a little thing but one which says a lot about Parkinson's character and about the sense of fellowship the Granada days generated.

I happened to be in the bar at BBC Television Centre at the time he had his chat show which was making his face one of the best known in television. In the corner of the bar sat a very high powered group of BBC executives, the top flight of the Beeb's management alongside a small cluster of celebrities and Michael Parkinson. As I stood there at one end of the bar I looked across, waved a quick hello and carried on drinking. But within a minute he had left his own party and came over to me for quarter of an hour to ask what I was doing and to recall some of the days when we had worked together. And all this in a natural way without any distance or phoney stardom.

[103]

Towards the end of 1962 the revolution which had been brewing in Liverpool was beginning to explode onto the rest of the world. One evening, with no fanfare of advance publicity, the Beatles, then little known by more than a handful of fans from the Cavern days, turned up at the studios for an appearance on Scene at Six Thirty. There was no fuss and no call to recruit extra security men at the door. They created little interest other than by their startling hair cuts and high fashion 'gear'. To me it seemed reassuring that the rest of the country, 'Granadaland' at least, was taking notice of what Liverpool had to offer. One of the producers at Granada seemed alarmed that the Beatles were intent on performing one of their own songs. 'Isn't Rogers and Hammerstein good enough for you?'

It was beginning to strike me as more and more ironic that I had spent so long trying to cover the traces of my Scouse accent only to see it attaining the status of high fashion. Over the following months that Scouse revolution became a stampede and each time the Beatles were due to make an appearance at the studios a large army of young kids would besiege that building. Screaming teenagers would rattle on the railings and chant slogans outside the building as traffic came to a virtual standstill in the street below.

On one memorable evening in the studio I was the newsreader on Scene at Six Thirty, Michael Parkinson and Mike Scott were the presenters and the Beatles were the guests. It did not feel like a historic moment at the time but it was marvellous to hear those rough, anarchic Liverpool voices. Their accents were those I knew and loved and it felt as if the new generation, of which I was a member, had reached the battlements and was taking the citadel by sheer force of presence. We were here to be noticed.

A group of us formed up into a little gang and lived the life of O'Riley. Today we would have been known as the 'Brat Pack' but in those more innocent days we called ourselves the 'Young Tigers'. It sounds very quaint now, especially as we are in middle age and our roar has grown rather hoarse over the years. Many of us are still in the 'media' – in TVS, Granada, or ATV and elsewhere – so the experience was a grounding for professional life not just a flash in the pan. And whatever else it was, it was exciting. I adored the announcing work and outside the studio I was spending wild nights in Manchester clubs and lost week-ends in big houses in Cheshire. At the time I was sure our generation could change the world. I seemed to be having too good a time, though, to know quite how.

Many of the classic shows were in their infancy then and I was there, usually out of vision, where I was content to be, providing commentary and voice-over. 'All our Yesterdays' with Brian Inglis was a long running, modern history documentary series which had a loyal following and established a wide repu-tation for itself and its presenter. 'What the Papers Say', an irreverent look at stories as reported in the press, was able to blend humour, social comment, and hard-edged critical opinion in a programme which attracted something of a cult following.

I particularly enjoyed the voice work on 'What the Papers Say' because it had to be fast, crisp and precise. When it went well – which it almost always did – the announcers working on it got a real kick. The broadcast was live, of course, and demanded split second timing plus a certain intonation and delivery which could inject just the right amount of brio into an apparently neutral script. I could never fathom out why they put a producer with a dreadful stutter in charge of such a tight show. The readers, Peter Wheeler, Brian Trueman and I, received our cues down headphones. The presenter, always an established journalist, would introduce the programme and then up came the caption, a blown up copy of the newsprint itself in a very distinctive style. The voice down the headphones would crackle, 'C . . . C

. . . C . . . C . . . Cue Ray!' and off I would go with the result that a couple of seconds could go by before any voice accompanied the text. It became something of an unwritten rule that we bypassed the formal instruction and played the whole show by ear.

And when the day comes for reviewing the early shows of the classic 'University Challenge' it will be my voice that future generations will hear. I remember the routine so well. When one of the clever dicks, some of whom were older than me, pressed his buzzer I would scream out 'Quartbottle – Sheffield!' and the camera would zoom in to pick up quite impressive displays of erudition. For some reason they placed me at the back of the studio, perched high on a rostrum in what looked like a canvas tent. This may have had something to do with sound balance but it made me look as if I had contracted some terrible disease or had gone into purdah. I had no objection to staying out of sight on TV but it was surely taking things a bit far to screen me off from the real world when we were all together in the studio!

The company owned a little aircraft, a De Havilland Dove, which would often commute to London ferrying VIP's to meetings and shows. I managed to get a flight on it once when I was chosen to be the voice introducing a musical special called 'An Evening with Jacques Brel' which we were to record in Granada's London base, the Chelsea Palace in the King's Road. This was the first time I had worked on such a prestigious programme and the first time, too, I had worked as a broadcaster in London. Such a combination of circumstance made for a large degree of nervous anticipation. It was also the occasion I learnt what was to be my single most important lesson in this game.

Part of my role was to read out the opening titles. 'Ladies and Gentlemen, from the Chelsea Palace, Granada salutes the talents of one of France's greatest men of music, in an evening with Jacques Brel.' Simple enough. But, perhaps because I was overawed by the size of the theatre or the grandeur of the occasion, my delivery at rehearsal was judged to be grossly sub-standard, sounding more like a whispered apology for an event which we at Granada were trying to keep quiet and wanted no-one really to be listening to. The director ran up to me screaming. His words have echoed round my head ever since and his advice (to put it courteously) has been my watchword ever since. 'That was bloody awful', he bellowed, 'You sound like you're ashamed of the show. For God's sake give the thing some balls. Believe every word as if you'd learnt it at your grandma's knee and announce it as if you're giving advance warning of the Second Coming!'

Whenever I have been voicing some tedious award ceremony or beauty contest I have been conscious that I had to invest them with a sort of frantic enthusiasm, no matter how trivial the subject. It may sound over the top when used as part of normal conversation but on television it is essential to play it up in proportion to the medium itself. This was especially true of the Miss World Contest when for years I used to open the show by booming, 'The lure of the crown! Sixty nine of the world's most beautiful girls competing in London at the Royal Albert Hall for the coveted title, Miss World 1976!' The crown always had a lure, the title was always coveted, and the girls were, invariably, the most beautiful. Whether any of this was true was neither here nor there.

I thought of myself as the cover of a book. Slick and attractive to make you want to read the text and, on certain shows which I shall not name, providing a tough and professional enough binding to ensure all the pages did not fall out.

The process is also rather like selling. No matter how rough he feels, the guy who has the job of saying, 'Tonight, live from London . . .' has to make it sound as if it is the most exciting thing he has ever done in his life. It seems simple but it has a subtlety I was still learning when my career ended. There is

[107]

scope for some personality but only so much. Too little and your blandness is a switch-off, too much and they start asking, 'Who's more important? Ray Moore or Jacques Brel?' When you get it right you frame the programme and enhance it without drawing attention to yourself. And only when you are not there or when you do it badly does the audience realise how important your job really is.

Such a realisation was now beginning to dawn on my father who bought a television set simply because I was on it, installed it in a prominent spot in the living room, and never tired of mentioning in 'casual' conversation at the pub that this was his son, 'He's on the television, you know'. The arrival of the TV set was the only new development at home. Don was still doing well at school, studying hard to qualify many years later as an electronics boffin on the NASA space programme. Jan had started work in one of the local banks and our house was a model of normality and domestic calm. All the clouds which had hung over the household in previous years were beginning to lift and Dad could walk into a pub without disappearing for three days at a time. And whenever I was in Liverpool I was usually at his side paraded as the object of affection and pride.

If he had ceased to be the source of eccentric events in the home, he continued to be caught up in them, strangely attracted to the extraordinary, as a moth to a flame.

He had gone over to the Isle of Man, for instance, one summer's weekend in '63 to see his ageing relations. On the day he was due back I had been in the front room writing letters, enjoying a brief few days at home. It was a scorching afternoon and because the sash on the window had broken I had propped it up with a box of Swan Vestas. At tea time I cycled to the pier head to meet Dad off the boat. He had obviously had a convivial crossing and was ruddy-faced, beaming and beery. But he was as good humoured as he always had been, if in a fuzzy kind of way. By now, of course, I was old enough to understand him better and, because familiarity with the effects of alcohol had made me less afraid of their real implications, I took him in hand and steered him tenderly in the direction of home where normality and balance awaited him. We arrived to find a scene of mayhem, and chaos.

Three fire engines were parked outside the house. Dozens of firemen moved in and out, one with a fire hose playing gently on the front room window. The paraphernalia of the emergency services were strewn about the street as visitors from miles around gathered to watch the fun. The front room sash window was horribly charred. I could barely comprehend the scene but what Dad, slightly the worse for wear and newly arrived on home ground, could make of it I dared not think. I called to mind the 'Drunkard's Nightmare', a popular seaside tableau, which for the price of a penny depicted the horrific visions visited on wayward boozers by way of calling them to temperance. My father quickly sobered up to be told the rational explanation and to be reassured that fiery retribution was not to be laid at his own door now.

Evidently Mum had gone to the open window, removed the Swan Vestas, which in the afternoon sun had been nearing flash point. Slight movement had caused ignition and the whole box had set the net curtains alight. In no time at all the window was completely ablaze. Dad swayed quietly and viewed the scene with bemused detachment. His words were singularly appropriate, 'No harm done', he mumbled. I returned to Manchester shortly after, for a quieter life.

At the time Granada was on the air only from Monday to Fridays. A long gone company called ABC took over at the weekends. Even so the Granada region, or Granadaland as it was called then, was vast compared to regional networks today. It covered the whole of Lancashire, Yorkshire, bits of

Lincolnshire and the Lake District and a strip along the coast of North Wales to Anglesey. It was an enormous empire which they occasionally split for transmission purposes, so that different commercials could go out in Lancashire and Yorkshire at the same time.

The arrangement was particularly useful to me. If I had an appointment I needed (or wanted) to break I simply said I was working. When, on more than one occasion, a current girlfriend challenged this by claiming that I could not have been working because she had been watching television all night and had not seen or heard any trace of me, I simply claimed territorial immunity, 'I was doing the commercials for the Yorkshire region', I would lie, 'that's why I wasn't on'. It was a perfect excuse I used to get me away from many a nasty hole.

The addiction to the medium induced a craving which could not be satisfied. I dreaded the weekends when the studios went dark and looked for extra work which would tide me over until Monday when my routine would begin again. I managed to get a relief announcer's job on Saturday and Sunday with Tyne Tees Television, so now my working week became a continuous loop. On Fridays I finished early at Granada, caught the train to Newcastle and spent the weekend in in-vision continuity, linking the programmes. Tyne Tees seemed to attract very few commercials in those days and so, unlike today when advertising space is snapped up, there were whole minutes to fill between each network show. The arrangement led to some very odd bits of broadcasting along the lines of, 'And now a look ahead to our programmes three weeks on Thursday'.

On Sunday afternoons matters would get so desperate that I started doing birthday requests for children to fill up the time and would sit there grinning as I said, 'Happy Birthday, Jimmy, in Newton-Aycliffe. Happy Birthday, Joan, in Seahouses'. It was an embarrassing ordeal even for me to perform. I cannot imagine what the viewers made of it. Strangely enough I saw something very similar on BBC Children's TV, the other day.

The weekend over, I caught the Monday morning train to Manchester for another five days with Granada. The arrangement meant that I was now on the air for seven days every week. And I loved it. I was greedy for experience, trying to pack into my working week more than the normal shift system would allow and searching out new duties to satisfy this craving.

It was during this period, in the autumn of 1964, that my announcing partner, Bernard Youens, left the continuity suite for the studio floor and our inventive system came to an end. Coronation Street was expanding and creating new characters to people that ever popular series. The latest was a rough, but likeable, layabout called Stan Ogden. When it was suggested Bernard should audition he surprised himself by landing the part. The Street was by now established enough to offer the prospect of long term employment and gave Bernard the opportunity to develop his talents as a character actor in a part he was to invest with personal warmth and humour and make his own. He kept the part for twenty years, until his death in 1984.

I, too, was considering change. Not only was the routine I had established a tiring one but it was beginning to offer no new challenge. It was something I could do in my sleep and, given my long hours, sometimes did. I asked myself seriously what my ambition was and realised that it had not changed. The BBC was still the aim so perhaps I should consider moving further south to achieve it. Perhaps because I was still bruised from my last experience of metropolitan life I opted for a compromise and moved half way, to Birmingham, where I was given an in-vision announcing and newsreading job with ATV. The studios were at Aston, a wonderfully glamorous location, surrounded on one side by the HP Sauce factory, on the other by Ansell's Brewery and, on the third, by a gas works. The great attraction of working here was that you always knew from which direction the wind was blowing.

The job was, however, a disappointment. It involved sitting in front of the camera, like a well-groomed tailor's dummy, grinning without reason and mouthing clichés; parroting someone else's was a double indignity. Appearing nightly on the programme, young and not bad looking, also had a dreadful effect on my personality. I began to believe my publicity and foolishly thought I was someone extremely important. I became vain and self-centred, but had at least the intuition to realise it and to want to change it. Soon after I arrived in Birmingham I began looking for ways to leave. In the summer of 1965 the opportunity arose.

That year BBC2 had opened in London and the Midlands and was due to be launched in the north of England in the late autumn. I saw a job advertised by the BBC in Manchester, for a person to write and shoot short promotional films to publicise the arrival of the new channel. In addition, the job would entail what were described as 'a certain number of announcing duties'. It seemed tailor made for me. OK, it wasn't London but it was the BBC, and if the Corporation would not let me in through the front door, then why not creep in through the tradesmen's entrance in Manchester, while nobody was looking? There was only one drawback to this plan. I had never written or shot a promotional film in my life. Untroubled by this apparent disqualification, I applied self-confidently for the job.

When the day of the interview arrived Mum and Dad had decided to come along as well to offer me support. By now, of course, Dad was completely won over to my way of life and was giving me tips on how best to impress the interviewers. This was it. The big moment, the culmination of twenty years of hoping and longing. As the three of us sat in the sunshine in Piccadilly Gardens, half an hour before the appointment, no-one spoke. I think Mum and Dad knew the importance of the event for me and it needed no elaboration. My nerves were infectious and the tension that hung over our part of the garden was almost palpable. Mum and Dad wished me luck and I set off.

Broadcasting House in Manchester was then a tall, grey stone building, standing right on Piccadilly, the letters BBC emblazoned on the top floor facade. I looked up at the letters in awe and made my way through the door – through the door, at last – to a room on the fourth floor where a large, balding man sat smiling behind a large desk. This was David Willmott, Presentation Organiser. I told him what I had done and he seemed impressed. I was honest about my lack of experience filming but he surprised me by seeming to take little notice of my weaknesses and concentrating on my strength, which was announcing, about which we talked at length. The interview drew to a familiar close as he thanked me and promised to get in touch. All I really wanted to ask was, 'When do I start?', but I thanked him and joined my parents outside.

A week later confirmation of what I had quietly suspected arrived at our house. I had felt that the interview had gone well and the letter from Manchester proved it. I was in. It was only a three month contract but three months with the BBC had to be better than three years as the Cheshire Cat on ATV.

On my first day I was met by David Willmott and taken, in the old clanking lift, up to the Presentation Office. As I was talking to one of the secretaries, Margaret Davis, a portly, middle-aged lady, who wore glasses on a string round her neck, and sat behind a cast-iron typewriter, the door opened and a young woman came in. She was older and more sophisticated than I was and pretty enough to turn my head immediately. I looked into her dark eyes for longer than I should have, and realised that something in them excited and frightened me. Her fair hair was framed by the upturned collar of her shag-piled coat. Then someone said, 'Ray, would you like to meet Alma?'

[7]

If my first day began on a high note with a romantic flourish, it descended rather quickly into a hazy farce.

I was to be working initially under the guidance of a chap called John Marten. When I met him he was sitting in the TV continuity suite in front of an enormous bank of switches, faders, buttons and flashing lights. Beyond that was a rack of half a dozen television monitors. It was bigger than anything I had seen before at Granada and ATV and the technology was beginning to frighten me. I felt sure that merely mastering the controls was going to take as long as my contract had to run and any trace of the overconfidence of my Birmingham days was wiped away immediately. The set-up here was immense and filled me with genuine dread forcing me to question whether I was really up to it. And if I failed; if I proved unequal to the challenge I had set myself, what then? I had better get down to work straight away.

John Marten had other plans. He was a curious chap with a careworn look and rheumy eyes. He gave the constant impression of a little boy lost in a crowd. As time passed I often felt like putting my arm round him and giving him a word of fatherly advice. For the moment, though, he was in charge in his uniquely easy going sort of way. He began a cursory explanation of the workings of this gigantic control panel and fielded a few of my questions with an air of distraction. I persisted with my curiosity but it was clear that his mind was on other matters. It was approaching eleven o'clock and his fidgetiness was galvanised into resolve as he suggested we get a breath of air and resume our discussion elsewhere.

The back of Broadcasting House, where we made our way via the clanking lift, presented a very different impression from that of its grand Piccadilly facade. The filthy alleyway behind was lined with bins full of rotting food which the pigswill men were loading on to a lorry up ahead. John led the way, negotiating the grease and the refuse, into a scruffy looking pub which blended perfectly into the background. With a nod to what were obviously the regulars we took our places in a cosy, if rather grubby, snug at the rear of the bar.

Eleven am on a Monday morning of a working week seemed an odd time to be downing pints of Chesters bitter but the arrangement was well suited to John who enlisted my support there and then as drinking partner and shoulder-to-cry-on. We chatted pleasantly about our lives and John regaled me with harrowing tales of his time in Associated Rediffusion in London and at ATV in Birmingham, painting a picture of a life which seemed to be littered with personal and professional trauma.

Time went on and an unlikely parade of Hogarthian ragamuffins filed in and joined us in the snug, men with unexplained names like the 'Duke of Fullers Earth', and 'Nobby the Fire'. The room filled with ex-policemen, bookmakers' runners, and assorted market stall-holders, reeking of fish.

I suggested to John that perhaps we had better get back to the studio but he confidently dismissed such misguided notions on the grounds that I could learn as much about the job sitting in the pub as I could in the studio. Even to a rather junior recruit this seemed an unorthodox attitude to take but, as I was nominally under the man, I decided I had better go along with it. It became obvious quite quickly that, of John's many personal qualities, the ability to be a serious contender for an Olympic medal in the boozing arts figured prominently. The broadcasting world was capable of putting up stiff competition in this field of personal endeavour but in any match John could outdo most rivals. In quick sprints, marathon sessions, combination events, he could outshine all comers. His chosen field was a sort of drinker's pentathlon which could draw bonus marks for style. He was not satisfied with beer and Guinness but went for a mixture of everything else. A large scotch would be chased down with a green Chartreuse, an egg nog jostled with a blue Bols, and a gin and cin rubbed shoulders with pints of cider. John never had his 'usual' in his life. Each day was a new experiment, the occasion to try ever more elaborate combinations. It was a frightful waste of money because whatever he drank (and in whatever permutation) would not affect him in any way except to make him a little slower and more deliberate and to cause his eyes to water rather more.

As we shuffled out of the bar into the alleyway which by now had been cleared but looked just as filthy as before, John suggested that my training for the day was pretty much complete and, since there was little for me to do in the afternoon, I might just as well go home. By this time I was decidedly past my sell-by-date and considered it a reasonable suggestion. Only as I was walking away did it strike me that this whole experience was rather odd. This was, after all, my first day in the BBC and the moment I had prayed for all my life. And what had happened on this momentous day? I had spent forty minutes in the studio, four hours in the pub and was now swaying back home at tea-time decidedly under the weather. This was not quite what I had expected.

As I got to know John better I realised that he was a professional at heart despite the outside appearances. One thing he did teach me was to have a healthy disrespect for the medium. No bad thing, perhaps, to tell someone as starry-eyed as me. Be professional, yes; do it right, yes; but remember that in the end most of it is only entertainment and there are many other things in life, infinitely more important. As an eager 23 year old I was in no mood then to listen to his advice and it is only now, now that my career is at an end, that the real wisdom of his remarks becomes apparent.

On the Tuesday morning I got down to serious work. Mastering the intricacies of a control panel which seemed to have a wayward mind of its own was the first priority. I then tried to make a tentative start on organising a film crew to go and shoot these short commercial trailers. I was fumbling in the dark asking obvious questions of everyone I met from secretaries to producers. Slowly, as these things always do, it settled into place and, confidence resumed, I could feel at ease in the work.

Alma Mather, I later discovered, did not work in Presentation at all, but in the offices next door. She was the BBC Gramophone Librarian, responsible for tracking down and issuing discs for use on the whole range of radio and TV programmes. She was a lively, skittish sort of girl with a great sense of teasing fun. All the men seemed to like her and she used to flirt shamelessly with all of them, which, for some reason, irritated me. Ours was a relatively small set-up and as the grams library and Presentation were side by side we would all meet up quite frequently for a drink. It wasn't too long before I was meeting Alma on her own and dropping in at the BBC club after work, where it was clear I was enjoying her company enormously.

One of the announcer's roles at the time was to act as a kind of Duty Officer in the evening, someone on hand to answer calls, mostly complaints, from viewers. This was the time of pioneering drama, risqué plays, and irreverent reviews. It was all very shocking for some people and on occasions viewers would telephone in their hundreds. Very often, though, the remarks showed a certain double standard. One I treasure involved a man who had watched a particularly compelling contemporary drama and was moved to voice his opinion after he had taken the trouble to sit through it in its entirety. 'Did you see that play?' he inquired innocuously enough. 'I wish to complain about the f..... language that was used. Call that filth a play. It's a f...... disgrace.' Many a time callers wanted to get involved in a long and rambling chat about the whole ethos of the BBC and I would be reluctantly drawn in to defending everything from 'Muffin the Mule' to 'Play for Today'. If total exasperation threatened I used to bring the conversation to a close by asking them to quote their TV licence number at which point very often the line would go mysteriously dead.

Variety characterised the work then, and, in addition to operating the TV console and making the continuity announcements, I managed to do more work for the radio side of the operation. Increasing specialisation nowadays has meant that jobs such as the one I had at the time no longer exist in quite that form, so I count myself fortunate to have been able to alternate between two very different media with such ease. The radio work involved reading the Northern news at lunchtime and teatime including a special bulletin for the Cumbrian and Manx edition. Nothing much happened among the crags and fells of those parts of the world because I remember reading out endless inconsequential titbits that overshadowed even the most serious item of national news: bicycles stolen from outside pubs in Peel on the Isle of Man, missing dogs in Whitehaven and characters being fined five pounds for being drunk in charge of a horse. There was never any evidence that people actually heard these bulletins and certainly no known reaction from those they were aimed at. Even so I could not help but wonder, as I read out the Manx bulletin, if somewhere on the Isle of Man, old 'Uncle' Harry, slumped in his armchair by the range, just might switch on from time to time and hear a voice he just might recognise as young Ray's. What he would make of it I could only guess.

I enjoyed the radio work more than the TV. It always seemed to me that the technology of the thing came between performer and viewer. With radio it was me, the microphone and the listener, an extraordinarily intimate relationship. I have always found that the lights, the wires, the cameras, the technicians, the make-up girls, were a barrier to communication and consequently have never felt entirely at ease within it. That is why I have such an admiration for people like Terry Wogan, with whom I worked in tandem much later on Radio 2. He could move effortlessly between radio and TV and emerge as master of both, giving just as much of himself in front of a crowded, bustling TV audience as he did in the silence and intimacy of a radio studio.

As my involvement with radio increased, I was given my very first record show, a pretty pathetic affair by any standards, amounting to a ten minute filler between programmes entitled, with great wit and verbal ingenuity, 'Just a Little Moore'. The great challenge to a radio presenter is to make music and comment flow naturally together, to assemble a structure without joins and allow the listener the impression that disparate elements have fused luxuriously into one. At the best of times this is not easy but under the conditions we had at Manchester this ideal remained impossibly out of reach.

We had a studio with one turntable. This is a major disadvantage, since a minimum of two is required to enable the presenter to set up the next record, while the first is playing and so leave him free to introduce it without having to worry about getting the vinyl disc out of the sleeve, dropping it on the floor or spilling his coffee over it. So with one turntable, away I go. The record ends and I begin to chat casually while lifting it off the turntable and selecting a replacement. I check it is the right one, still chatting away, and put it on hoping to God that the stylus, which is by now shaking in my hand, will land somewhere near the start of the music. Often it does not and there follows a yawning gap, during which the regular scratches are audible. Sometimes the stylus overshoots and bounces in on Enrico Caruso in full flood half way through an operatic aria. It must have made a bizarre listening experience.

In order to select my records, of course, I needed the services of the grams librarian. Very soon Alma and I found ourselves huddled in the library, compiling these ten minutes extravaganzas together. Each week it took us longer and longer to complete as we were by now not wholly concentrating on the work. Something rather serious and unspoken was going on between us. She was thirty at the time and I twenty three, an age gap which would be irrelevant today but which, then, in a pre toy-boy era, was rather shocking. Worst of all she was married and had a son aged nine. We both tried to push this from our minds, with only limited success.

We were now meeting not only for a drink after work, but at lunchtime too. We would leave the building at different times and by different doors then together we would set off for one of the parks nearby to eat our sandwiches. It was all very quaint and innocent but we were definitely falling in love. In fact I had fallen in love with her much, much earlier. We tried to keep the lid on things and keep it from the rest of the office. We thought we were being very discreet about things but the whole world knew. Apart from Alma's husband, Roy. We never met at weekends but the long hours we spent at work almost made up for that. And they were long hours. I had to spend a lot of time in the library selecting the records and Alma would often pop into the continuity studio drinking coffee, delivering my discs by hand and teasing me.

One day I got a call from the Light Entertainment producer, John Wilcox, who told me he was mounting a brand new pop radio show for the network. The Beatles phenomenon was having its knock-on effect throughout the whole of the music world and people were taking more risks with popular taste. Even straight-laced 'Auntie' had to loosen her stays. The show he had in mind was to be called 'Pop North', to cash in on the regional renaissance, and would enlist the services of the Northern Dance Orchestra and assorted star guests every week. He thought I might like to introduce it. With a mixture of excitement and blind panic I said yes. I knew I had never attempted anything remotely like it before – there had never *been* anything remotely like it before – but after a long career agreeing first and assessing the decision later I consented on the spot. It had the added bonus of being a network show. Ray Moore was about to make his appearance on the Light Programme at last.

It was a whole new world to me and enormously entertaining. I had swapped the windowless continuity suite for the concert platform and up on stage as MC for an hour, introduced Hermann's Hermits, Freddie and the Dreamers, Gerry and the Pacemakers and dozens of the other big names of the time. It was a thrill to hear myself on the 'proper BBC', if only for an hour every Thursday lunchtime. Most weeks Alma came to the recordings and we stayed on long after everyone else had gone. Sooner or later I felt that her husband was going to start asking serious questions. I did not know it at the time, but he already had.

Whatever Alma and I did, we did not do lightly. It started as spontaneous affection, one for the other, and grew into something infinitely more substantial. Our being together felt right and natural but such convictions did little to dispel the guilt we both felt. A number of times we made the conscious effort to call things off but the feelings between us were too strong. We resolved, for her husband's and her son's sakes, to stop seeing each other and, for a time, it seemed to work. Alma withdrew from me and spent her time at work with her own friends. But even that strategy failed. We might go to the club separately only to see each other across the room, where our eyes could not fail to meet. Alma made two or three attempts to make her marriage work but she was fighting a battle she was destined to lose.

It was a cruel and painful time for both of us. Part of me knew it was morally wrong to be causing Alma to betray her husband in this way and yet another part of me knew equally well that the marriage was not a blissful one anyway and this was just the latest of a series of rocky patches it had hit. Her husband was a very successful businessman and was so occupied with his work that he had not been able to see what was going on under his nose – that he and Alma were slowly drifting apart and beginning to lead two separate lives. They had just grown at different rates and in different directions. He was in the building trade, a solid down-to-earth world which was far removed from the rather glamorous life Alma had now been drawn into at the BBC, mixing with actors and musicians and faintly irresponsible people, I suppose, who were determined to enjoy these exciting times. I often reasoned, in my saner moments, that the marriage would not have lasted even if I had not appeared on the scene. They would still have grown apart. The real dilemma and pain surrounded David, her son, whom she loved dearly. Surely it could not be right for me to tempt Alma away from him. It was when I reviewed that aspect of this affair that the guilt and the shame hit me full in the face. And yet all the time, pulling me in a contrary direction, was this inescapable truth; that Alma and I were by now deeply and unmistakably in love.

At moments of emotional crisis in my life I have consistently employed the same life-saving technique. To throw myself into work with even greater effort. My private life may be in a mess, I thought, but at least I have the satisfaction of knowing that my professional life is rock solid. Inexperienced, immature, irresponsible I may be in matters of the heart, I said to myself, but when it comes to broadcasting I know where I am.

The sheer variety of work managed to take my mind off the sadness. No more ridiculous contrast to the high drama of my emotional life could be imagined than a strange little programme which I introduced on Friday evenings. It was called 'Fisherman's Corner' and starred a delightful character called Hal Mount, who would pretend to be enclosed in some mossy hollow on the river bank. Sound effects discs of babbling brooks played in the background while Hal would puff on his pipe and exclaim, 'Good Heavens, a 10 lb pike!' At this point effects men would begin to tread water to provide the appropriate atmosphere and Hal would chip in with another, 'My word, and is that a roach over there, too?' Every week within the space of ten minutes he caught at least five magnificent fish with a flourish of tomfoolery which hoodwinked no-one. In a Freudian slip one week, I introduced him as Hal Roach.

One week I found myself introducing a recorded programme featuring the ventriloquist Ray Allen, who with his puppet, Lord Charles, has established himself as one of the classic acts of modern British variety. I sat to stage right, providing opening and closing announcements and presenting the various acts as they came on stage. I introduced Ray Allen and sat back to enjoy the performance when I suddenly broke out into a sweat. There was only one microphone on stage and yet there were two people speaking. I rushed up to Ray and apologised to the audience and said we would have to start again because we had not provided a microphone for Lord Charles. Ray looked at me in disbelief – a microphone for a dummy? – and then, red faced, I realised my mistake. The audience laughed, clearly thinking it was part of the act, but Ray was not amused nor, I imagine, was Lord Charles.

I was required to be the BBC's man for all occasions and introduced, from time to time, symphony concerts performed by the BBC Northern Orchestra. Manchester was very much a cultural centre, despite any southern prejudice to the contrary, and music was its strong suit. We recorded the programmes in a dark, cold cavern of a place called the Milton Hall on Deansgate. These were tense moments because what you might just get away with with Lord Charles, you most certainly would not with Sir John Barbirolli, who was frequently the guest conductor at these sessions. To the guys in the orchestra he was known as Bob O'Reilly, but I had no such endearments to know him by. His formal presence used to intimidate me somewhat. Unfortunately the pieces of music chosen were often completely unknown to me and I could not always remember what point the music had reached. I lived in mortal fear that I would launch into my closing announcement before they had played the final movement.

For obvious reasons all the shows were timed to the second. It is no use, for example, having a first rate programme overrunning by one minute and thirty seconds. For one thing, if time is precious, and another show is waiting to go on the continuity announcer may just be forced to slice the minute and a half off the end and thereby make a nonsense of it. Another reason is that at fixed points in the day the familiar pip, pip of the Greenwich time signal is programmed to play automatically. Six loud bleeps coming in during the closing prayer of the 'Daily Service' will not enhance the experience. And if everybody overshot by one minute – or even just by the thirty seconds – the programmes would be starting at unpredictable times and no-one would be able to plan an evening's listening. There is another compelling reason, too. And that is that, when dealing with live musicians, a mis-timing can lead into overtime which according to Musicians' Union rules has to be paid for at the full going rate. Having to pay a twenty piece band overtime is a powerful incentive on a producer to get his timings right. I was involved one night in a memorable race against the clock, when the producer had got them wrong.

It was a live late night show, involving a full scale orchestra and a number of guests. As usual I introduced them and gave the closing announcements. The musicians were paid the normal rate, providing the show did not go past ten o'clock. A second after and it was double time and a programme budget blown sky high. The programme got off to a good start but towards the end the producer came up to me in a panic, 'Look, Ray, we've got a problem', he said, 'We're going to be over.'

'By how much?' I asked.

'About thirty seconds', he replied. Not much, but enough to take the minute hand into the magic quadrant. By now the band had started up on its last number and could smell panic, and extra cash, from the producer's box. Surprisingly enough they showed no signs of stepping up the tempo to help us out of a tight corner. We were now approaching the closing bars and the producer looked to me as his only hope. 'How long's your close?' he asked.

'Forty five seconds', came my reply.

'Right, cut out all the credits, forget the thank yous, and just wind it up as soon as you can before 10.'

The last chord sounded, the band sat down and a corporate grin settled in as they turned their attention to me. The time: nine fifty-nine and forty-five seconds. They knew the closing routine well and were surprised to hear me starting it up at a slightly faster pace than usual. Then they registered that this was to be a perfunctory close indeed. I increased my speed to a tempo which would have been more appropriate to describing the final furlong of the Derby.

It was a lovely, carefree life, reading the news for an audience of sheep on the Isle of Man, hob-nobbing with Wayne Fontana, hosting disjointed record shows, quivering before Bob O'Reilly, and hosting a ludicrous series about imaginary fish. It was all too good to last.

In the summer of 1967 I got another break; the opportunity to make my first broadcast for the BBC in London. The presenter of one of the top-rated shows at the time, 'Saturday Club', was going on holiday for three weeks and the producer, Bill Bebb, thought it a good opportunity to try out a few possible replacements. I was chosen to do one of the shows. So I travelled to London and, at long last, entered Broadcasting House legitimately. I was now on the inside. Feeling ten feet tall I glided through the reception hall and down into the basement along miles of corridor to Studio B13. I remember constantly reminding the audience that they were listening to the Light Programme of the BBC – as if to convince myself that it was all really true.

I emerged into the sunshine in triumph as if I had scaled a huge mountain. Bill and I went round the corner to The George for a drink of celebration. This legendary establishment had been one of Dylan Thomas' legendary watering holes in the Fifties and even on that Saturday lunchtime it had a touch of the Bohemian about it. As I looked round Bill pointed out a number of people, putting faces to names I knew from the Radio Times. And now I, with one live network show behind me, felt part of this lovely world. To see my own name in Radio Times was thrilling enough. On my way back to Euston I made a small detour and walked past the cigarette shop where I had had such an inglorious four day career and I smiled with a deep sense of optimism.

I also felt immense pride that I was now one of the heirs to the legacy of the great Lord Reith, the BBC's first Director General and creator of public service broadcasting in Britain. I often reread stories of his life and respected the Corporation for embodying the values he held dear. It has rather gone out of fashion to expect the BBC to perform a moral duty to the nation, to set standards of integrity and behaviour, but I held those principles deeply then, and still do. I like to think that from the very beginning of my career I stuck to those guiding values, even in my flippant field of Light Entertainment. The notion that the BBC is there in a triple capacity – to inform, instruct, and entertain – has become, in some quarters, rather old fashioned, but it had (and has) a powerful hold on me.

But here, in the summer of 1967, was the very root of my dilemma. For all I might talk of ideals and honourable behaviour, as embodied by the BBC, I was still 'carrying on' with a married woman and that sort of behaviour would never have been tolerated by the first DG. It would have made little difference to protest my true love for her in self defence. I would be taking the risk of dragging down the BBC's good name and reputation. And that is what I felt I was doing though I loved Alma so much that I could never leave her now.

There had been unpleasant scenes outside Broadcasting House in Manchester already. Alma's mother had lain in wait for me one evening and, having given me more than a fair share of her anger, had set about me with her handbag, clouting me over the head until I could make a discreet escape. How I could make it discreet with half of Piccadilly looking on I do not know. I simply fled. My parents, too, had got to hear of this somehow and were full of anger and condemnation. Having got so far and done so well, how could I ruin it all like this? I had no answer save to say I was powerless to resist my emotions and I had found someone who put pure ambition in the shade. The whole thing threatened to become a public scandal. The headlines were clearly in the making, 'Young newsreader runs off with married woman'. It never made the local papers but it was threatening to, so I decided I would have to resign from the

BBC to save them any potential embarrassment. I gave a month's notice, thinking that the most dramatic thing was over. There was one more shock to come.

Alma, during this time, had decided there could be no turning back from what she knew she had to do. One Wednesday morning she came to work with a small bag packed and told me, suddenly and simply, she had left home for good. She looked frightened and vulnerable and I felt doubly guilty for all the tears I had caused.

We had both sacrificed everything for each other. Alma had given up a comfortable home, a husband and her beloved son, and I had walked away from the very thing I had ached for all my life, the BBC. We had each other but it was a very unfriendly world which the two of us were now preparing to face.

The implications of our decision were shattering. I was a young man used to having no responsibilities; the archetypal bachelor, footloose and fancy-free. But now, suddenly, I was responsible for another human being. With no job, no prospects, no money to rely on I was, or so I thought, the unofficial breadwinner. I had a sinking feeling in the very pit of my stomach. I was nervous all day long, unable to view the future without trembling. I had nightmares of not being able to provide for Alma. I would wake up in the middle of the night and imagine her starving and me unable to buy enough food to keep us both. From being on the crest of a wave, where I could view the limitless horizon of promise and opportunity, I had fallen, at a stroke, into a deep trough, where the water towered so high that I thought we would never be afloat again.

I finished working for the BBC in Manchester at the beginning of September 1967. If I had been able to stand back from all this and been able to see, via some crystal ball, what was going on below the surface of these turbulent waters I would, at least, have had reason for some small optimism. Friendships and loyalties won over the past few years ensured that Alma and I, although now independent of the BBC, were not abandoned by close colleagues within it. Little did I know that kind friends were hard at work behind the scenes trying to find me a home, somewhere in the Corporation.

Our departure coincided with a major change in the network which was to have unpredictably favourable consequences for us. The Light Programme was on the verge of being split into two separate services. The first would be a pop music station, and the second a more middle of the road affair. They would be known respectively as Radio 1 and Radio 2.

Out of the blue and, as I judged at the time, totally undeservedly, I was offered a three month contract to help launch Radio 2 at the end of September. Nothing happens in the way you expect. Alma and I were almost penniless, close to homeless and yet, although I was unaware of it at the time, I was on the brink of achieving my lifetime's dream – a job as announcer and newsreader on the BBC in London. Alma had left home with little more than the clothes she stood up in and I, too, had very little to call my own, so we packed what few possessions we had and set off for London, which is where our new life together really started.

[8]

Life for the two of us did not start in style. When we arrived in London we took up residence in a seedy bed and breakfast hotel in Sussex Gardens, near Paddington Station. Even today, while the area offers refuge of a sort to the rootless, it provides a cheerless base for a couple starting out afresh. At the time it seemed more than ever to have been designed specifically to undermine our confidence, as though it sensed the desperation of its transitory inhabitants and relished it. Our hotel, no worse than many that surrounded us, was dreadful. An all pervasive smell of cooking fat hung in the air, sticking to clothes and hair and bedsheets. Moreover, staying there was not cheap and, as I had no job, our finances were dwindling fast. I got into the habit of staking out the bank, waiting until the manager left for lunch, and nipping in furtively to cash a cheque.

After a week or so we heard that Alma's husband wanted a serious chat with us both and this new development introduced an element of real fear into what hitherto had been merely black farce. From then on we had to leave the hotel to settle into another, and then another. I felt like the Scarlet Pimpernel constantly on the move, living out of suitcases and forever looking over my shoulder for Alma's husband or the bank manager. The horizon of our life was marked out by a series of tatty, greasy hotels in which we sought temporary shelter, unwilling or too cowardly to confront Alma's husband head on. We sometimes relive that trauma and wonder how we ever survived those times. Much that surrounds this painful period is deliberately hazy as both of us tried consciously to blot it all from our minds. Only the ties of affection kept us from going under and these, often against all the odds, have held good for over twenty years.

After a month of wandering and of questioning the wisdom of our decision we reached a point beyond which lay emotional and financial collapse. One miserable Friday evening, as we prepared to admit defeat, we were pulled back from the brink by a sudden brainwave. We both remembered a wonderful Cockney character, called Joe Fessey, who had worked as a wire-man for the BBC in Manchester for some months. Joe was as round as he was tall and had character and humour big enough to match. He and Alma used to flirt and tease constantly and I think he was a bit in love with her. He was based in London now, still working with the BBC and had said many times that if we were ever down we should give him a call and he would put us up for a few days. He doubtless had in mind a few days holiday, a casual break from the work routine rather than a quasi elopement which is what this virtually amounted to. In desperation we phoned him and from our tearful, muttered apologies he could tell we had reached the end of a long road. Decisively, warmly, and in a way we can never forget he took us both in hand, 'Go to the BBC Club', he said, 'I'll pick you up in an hour'.

We went to the meeting place and sat alone, sipping our halves of bitter like orphans while a jolly crowd celebrated the arrival of the weekend at the bar. Suddenly Joe's head and his portly frame filled the doorway and we scratched together loose change to buy him a gin and tonic. He was carrying bags of shopping; chicken, fruit, vegetables, bread, milk, a bottle of wine and a little posy of flowers for Alma. Of course we could stay with him! He bundled our suitcases into the back of a cab and we headed off through the rain to Pimlico.

Joe's place was in Churchill Gardens, an enormous modern housing development. The flat itself was tiny with a living room, a kitchen and a bathroom. He insisted that Alma and I take the two divans in the main room while he, at great inconvenience to himself, camped out in the kitchen. The three of us had a tremendous feast that night and Alma and I went to bed rested and secure at last, sensing that this was a watershed for us both.

Radios 1 and 2 were launched with trumpets and fanfares on September 29th, 1967. Our friends in Manchester had served us well. Their quiet lobbying had paid off and I started out on the life I had craved for so long, that of a BBC announcer based in Broadcasting House.

I arrived when the great giants of sound broadcasting still stalked the studios. I had revered these legendary men for so long and now here I was sharing the same announcers' common room. The behemoths were there when I strode in to take *my* place alongside them – Jimmy Kingsbury, Alvar Liddell, John Snagge, John Webster, Bruce Wyndham. It was, as Dag Hammarskjold had said in a different context, 'The proof of all you never dared believe possible'. Alvar in particular was very kind to me, giving me every encouragement I needed, and I, in return, could only marvel that I was now almost on equal terms with him.

I am not, by nature, a strong willed individual so when I look back at that glorious event which even now I find barely credible I wonder how it all happened. I take no credit for achieving it. It seemed (and still seems) as if the experience was already there, marked down in advance and waiting to be discovered, the Destiny towards which an inner voice seemed to be guiding me.

I took ownership of my pigeon hole in the Broadcasting House common room, my name sandwiched between those of Roger Moffat and Alexander Moyes, and got down to work. It was a varied life, reading the news and 'Today in Parliament' on Radio 4, occasionally introducing a symphony concert from the old Farringdon Hall, and even hosting a talent show on Radio 1 on Sunday afternoons.

My main commitment, and probably the reason why they found a place for me in London, was to a team of presenters on 'Breakfast Special' on Radio 2, an early morning music show on air every day from 5.30am until 9. The fact that I was doing much the same thing twenty years later may not indicate great progress.

The show gave us a refreshing freedom, three and a half hours on the air in front of a live microphone and virtually a licence to say anything we liked. Here was the opportunity to put a personal stamp on a show, to develop it any way we chose. It was a glorious ego trip for us all. We might not be the part of the BBC delegated 'to instruct and inform' but we did carry out the BBC's other mission, 'to entertain', and we worked hard to create a show which worked.

The announcers met socially, too, and Friday lunchtime in The George became a tradition that lasted years. They were great, boozy laughing sessions full of heavily embroidered stories of gaffes on air – stories like the announcer who, on a very late duty, was clearly exasperated by the dreary music programme he was introducing. He opened his microphone and in his best BBC tones said, 'Ladies and gentlemen welcome to (let's call it) Music Night'. This he did with true professionalism despite his personal prejudice. The music programme began and he inadvertently left his microphone open as he added, by now broadcasting his feelings to the world, 'The trouble with the late shift is that you have to listen to this bloody rubbish!'

Participants at the Friday lunchtimes varied from week to week but there was usually a hard core – Bruce Wyndham, Roger Moffatt, Peter Latham, David Symonds, Eugene Fraser

[133]

and, though feeling initially like the spectre at the feast, me. Drink was a powerful driving force for many of us and several of the announcers had worked out detailed timings of the route between the studio and the local pubs. The George was three minutes away, the Yorkshire Grey three minutes twenty five seconds, the Stag one minute forty and the Dover Castle four minutes. Inevitably this led, on occasions, to somewhat breathless newsreading. It was also something of a traffic hazard to have a succession of announcers weaving between the cars and darting backwards and forwards, pocket watch in hand, like the White Rabbit from Alice in Wonderland.

It was like being a member of some anarchic school with sixth formers barely toeing the line and stretching the rules to the full. I remember on one occasion being on a newsreading duty on Radio 2 which had bulletins every half hour. I read the midday edition and decided to pop over to the Club in the Langham – sadly no longer the BBC's outpost and soon to become a hotel – for a drink. It so happened that on that day the Queen was making an official visit to Broadcasting House and, as a result, Portland Place was packed with people awaiting her arrival. I shuffled through the crowds, had a quick pint in the Club but underestimated those critical timings. As I left to make my way back to the studio the police, in expectation of the Queen's imminent appearance, had closed the road and refused to let me across. It was now 12.20pm and I was beginning to panic. As the Queen's car edged up Portland Place and all heads craned to the right I decided it was make or break time and shot out across the road like a whippet from a trap in front of the Royal Party. I am sure Her Majesty was not amused but I did make it back to the studio by 12.28pm.

In those early days it was still very formal. The era of the dinner jacket at the microphone had long since gone but we newsreaders were expected then to wear a suit and certainly, without a suit, entrance to the Club was strictly barred. I remember one Bank Holiday going into BH (as Broadcasting House is affectionately known) wearing a rather natty denim safari suit. I blush to think I could ever be seen in one at all but they were all the rage then. It was not a cheap thing either and had set Alma and me back a few bob. It was a quiet day with no-one around so I thought I would be considered suitably dressed. I walked through the door only to be passed by one of my senior colleagues who looked at me and sneered, 'Coming to work in dungarees. Whatever next?'

The lunatics on Radio 1 might be allowed a bit of licence but we newsreaders were not. The newsroom at the time, I remember, was populated by much older men and women, many of whom had been there in the war and who were steeped in what were, in the context of the 60's, the rather old fashioned traditions of the BBC.

Half of me regrets their passing, too, and I fear the news – across all the media, not just the BBC – is moving rather too closely towards entertainment. In some spurious rush to hold its own in the ratings, the news presentation is in danger of becoming too frenetic, too dramatic and, sadly, too repetitive. The newsreader will say, 'There's been a major explosion in an old boot factory in Kuala Lumpur, here's Harold Hairbrush at the scene'.

And up comes Harold Hairbrush, 'Yes, here I am in Kuala Lumpur at the site of the old boot factory where there's been a major explosion. Now back to the studio'.

'Harold Hairbrush reporting from Kuala Lumpur and we'll have more on that old boot story in our later bulletin.'

During my early time in the news, the world was much taken up with the nasty little war in Biafra and so the daily bulletins were always peppered with the doings of Colonel Ojukwu, Patrice Lumumba and a character called Sir Abu Bakar

Tafewabalewa. The pronunciation of this chap's name gave us all endless problems and required endless rehearsals. One or two of the announcers took the easy option of referring to him matily as Sir Abu but I practised and practised until in the end I was beginning to dream of Sir Abu Bakar Tafewabalewa. I sailed confidently into the studio one day ready to impress, only to learn that he had been shot dead that morning and was never to feature in the bulletins again.

Wrestling with unpronounceable names was the least of my worries. Alma and I could obviously not stay with Joe forever and we now had to scour London for a place of our own. We explored dingy basements in Pimlico, pokey rooms in Maida Vale and a curious garret in Earls Court which boasted a washbasin in a wardrobe and a lavatory shared by fifty others stricken with serious incontinence.

One night we spotted a studio flat for rent in Blackheath – only a short walk from where we live now – but neither of us had the faintest idea where Blackheath was. I remembered some very funny articles by Michael Frayn in the Observer chronicling daily life there and judged it to be an attractive, faintly eccentric place to be. So we investigated the area and rented the flat, an airy little place just off the Heath. The £8 15s weekly rent was going to tax our resources to the limit but we needed a pleasant place to call ours. By now Alma had resumed her old job, this time in the Gramophone Library in Egton House, next to Broadcasting House, and for the first time in months, we were not counting every penny. When we first moved in I went mad and spent 10s 6d on a bottle of Lutomer Riesling and together we toasted our new home.

Carefree celebration was, however, premature. We were still evading Alma's husband who had had one showdown with me, involving a bit of a scuffle. I feared the worst. One afternoon it came to a head when Alma and I knew he had asked our landlord for the key to let himself into our flat. We, meanwhile, were almost in hiding in a pub nearby. I had to have it out with him once and for all so I left Alma shaking in the saloon bar while I, shaking, headed for the flat. All that was lying in wait for me was a pile of clothes which, on closer inspection, turned out to be Alma's, stacked neatly on the bed.

A wave of sadness mixed with guilt washed over me; the guilt compounded some time later by the fact that he had, knowing us to be short of money, transferred half of his and Alma's joint account into her own account so that we were solvent at last. I tormented myself with the mess I had made of things. Sure, there was the euphoria of finally doing the job I wanted but it had been bought at such an emotional cost and the whole experience was tempered by this lingering sorrow. For all that, though, I continued to think of emotional equations which showed that on balance we were right to be following our hearts. If Alma goes back to him, I reasoned, three people will be chronically miserable. If she stays with me then at least two people will be happy. If love is blind, it is desperately selfish.

The one element which did not add up in the equation, though, was David, Alma's son. When I stopped to think what I was doing, I thought I had taken leave of my senses. Perhaps I had. What did I know about the ties of family life? How could a young man like me understand the pain of a child separated from a parent? Perhaps, though, I understood more than I dared admit. And that knowledge made it all the harder to bear. I thought the best thing to do was to keep out of David's life altogether until he was old enough to ask his mother about me. I resolved to stay in the background even though his mother would return to Manchester on frequent occasions to see him. And that is what I did in preference to forcing myself on him. It contradicted any moral sense I had but I was impelled by the integrity of the feeling of being, quite simply, quite cruelly, in love. Our love became obsessive and, in the full knowledge of the hurt I was causing, it seemed right. When we were together we were like children, blissfully happy.

And time has vindicated the stand we took. Alma's husband married again and has two beautiful daughters. David, grown up and married now, has a young son of his own and together we have an excellent relationship. He is a very dear friend to me and he was one of the first people I felt able to confide in, when my disease was first diagnosed. I realise that, despite my crazy equations, you can never draw up a profit and loss account that will satisfy the Almighty – still less any cynics and stone-throwers – so all I can say, simply and truthfully, is that our love has endured. And so has our marriage.

When I first suggested marriage Alma was reluctant. Having had one disaster she did not want another but I persisted and eventually persuaded her. Her divorce had come through a year after we had left Manchester and a year after that, on the 9th of May 1969, we tied the knot.

We had good omens and bad. Parental disapproval was one of the greatest hurdles we had to clear. Once again the age gap seemed to shock people – and it was doubly shocking that the woman, not the man, should be the older partner. Not for the first time was Alma cast as the alluring seductress and I a mere gigolo. Even today I find the age business difficult to understand. I look at Alma, still youthful and energetic, check the face against the age as written in her passport and think, 'Am I really going to bed with a grandmother?'

The one good omen we recall with affection involved that most romantic of things – the electricity bill. When we settled into our Blackheath flat we had to feed a meter in the corner of the living room. One day I suddenly realised that its voracious appetite for one shilling pieces had slackened and that we had not fed it for a couple of days. As we were particularly hard up that winter we found ourselves ignoring the meter's digestive system altogether. When, at the end of the season, we realised we had been lit and heated from January to April, we decided that at least somebody up there was on our side.

Our wedding, when it finally took place, was a deliberately low-key affair. Money was still a problem, so I booked the cheapest mini-cab firm I could find to take us to Greenwich Register Office. A grubby looking Vauxhall made its way to the front door and we had to move the spare wheel, parked conveniently enough on the back seat, before we could make room for the two of us. This we did to the accompaniment of a monumental thunderstorm which was breaking round our ears and causing us both to lose control of our temper before we finally reached the Town Hall. Our witnesses were Joe Fessey, who had hauled us off the streets just in time, and his girlfriend, Jess.

I cannot now remember why, but none of us had a camera and so we have no photographic evidence of the great day. All the proof we needed was that we were there together, arm in arm on the Town Hall steps with good old Joe by our side to vouch for it.

Afterwards the four of us travelled up to the West End to a little French restaurant called The Marquis, there to gorge ourselves and make serious inroads into their wine cellar. I suggested a round of brandies to finish and called over the waiter. 'Bisquit?' he asked.

'Er, no thanks. No biscuits, just the brandy', I replied.

'But Bisquit, monsieur?' he persisted.

'No. I've told you. No biscuits, thank you, just four brandies.' The waiter, in exasperation, wandered off to bring our liqueurs convinced by now that poor Alma had landed herself the thankless task of accompanying a half wit to dinner.

My professional life by now was beginning to pick up. I had

branched out into doing the voice work for the trailers between programmes on BBC1 and was regularly working at Television Centre in my spare time. The only snag was that my Radio 2 contract expressly forbade me from working for anybody else so I hit on the ruse of working at the TV Centre under an assumed name. I borrowed a name from one of Dad's many relations on the Isle of Man and, for many years, I was Ray Moore on radio and Daniel Christian on television. Despite what the contract said I could not really believe that BBC TV was 'anybody else'; it was surely a partner not a rival.

At the Centre I resumed my acquaintanceship with dear John Marten, the man who had made my first day with the BBC in Manchester such an alcoholic haze. He was still engaged in a single handed mission to consumer-test the entire contents of the bar – whisky sours, pints of stout, pink gins, white rums, black and tans all in quick succession. He was now more rheumy eyed than ever and in a constant state of near financial collapse which he would express as being, 'A little low on funds, dear boy'. He explained to me that when he got really desperate he would toddle off to Sussex, to see his father, a retired vicar and life-long teetotaller, who, John assured me, 'was comfortable'. John would invariably cook lunch and prepare a dessert heavily laced with sherry which the old boy tucked into with gusto. After a couple of generous helpings of this heady trifle he would become rather expansive, sentimental . . . and a little bleary eyed. He would then scrutinise John's unkempt appearance and ask if money was tight at the moment. John would mutter something about 'inordinate outgoings this month' and father would reach for his cheque book to tide him over with a couple of hundred quid.

This ploy was repeated with increasing frequency as John's quest for liquid variety showed no signs of diminishing. I was sitting in the club at Television Centre one evening as John was making his by now familiar attack on lager, egg-nog, and potent bottles of Old Tom and thought he seemed more morose than usual. He left, complaining of feeling 'rather below par' and for the first time in his life went home before the bar closed. By midnight he was dead. Evidently, he had fallen down some stone steps the day before and had been walking round Television Centre unaware that he had a fractured skull. It was a sad end for a strange and haunted man.

It was life in Broadcasting House – the home of radio – rather than Television Centre which was really providing the nourishment I needed. To my newsreading and continuity duties I now added another role. With John Dunn and Paul Hollingdale I became a regular presenter of the 'Breakfast Special' show and drew enormous pleasure from it, despite the need to be staggering out in the pitch dark every morning to prepare the programme.

It was at this time, in the late 60's, that I met Terry Wogan for the first time. He was an established figure in Ireland and working with RTE, the Irish broadcasting network, and was coming over once a week to do a show called 'Late Night Extra'. I was first struck by his quiet self assurance and solid professionalism. It was clear that here was an immensely shrewd man, warm and witty, and a man totally in control of a huge creative talent. In this rather fragile world of fragile egos there is inevitably a certain suspicion of the newcomer but the two of us seemed to hit it off from the beginning. By now I had some solid experience behind me so I was less inclined to be awestruck by fellow professionals but right from the beginning I saw in Terry a far more than average talent.

He was bright, sharp, had the highest possible professional standards and did not suffer fools easily. When he was offered the afternoon show in 1969 I think I felt rather jealous. The envy did not last because I recognised that Terry and I, despite a great kinship which was to deepen and strengthen even more as the years went on, are two different personalities. I am more a heart-on-the-sleeve man, whereas Terry is more enclosed and self-contained, allowing only as much of the real Wogan to come through as he wishes. Both of us were ambitious at the time and in that simple respect resembled each other. But to become really successful you need to have that bit of steel in your make-up. Terry has it but I don't.

One of my favourite shows of the late 60's was called 'Ray Moore's Saturday Night' which would involve us in a live two hour broadcast from a dance hall or a nightclub somewhere. Quite often the show would come from The Old Granary in Bristol where from time to time Acker Bilk's band used to play. The man is one of the most quick witted guys in the business and a master of the one liner. One night after a show a blind man came up to Acker and said, 'I ran into you once in Guildford'.

'It wasn't my bloody fault!' said Acker.

During the broadcast, by way of giving the band a breather, I would climb on stage and interview Acker about his work and his busy touring schedule. 'Yes, it's a punishing life', he said, 'Take next week, for instance. On Monday we've got a Nurse's Ball, on Wednesday a Policeman's Ball, and on Friday a Lord Mayor's Ball. In fact it's all a load of . . . private functions!'

Our producer on these shows was usually Brian Patten from Bristol who made sure these occasions were non-stop entertainments, both on and off the air. We happened to be staying at the Castle Hotel in Taunton after a particularly successful show. After a string of nightcaps at the bar, Alma and I retired to bed. The following morning we were both aware of scuffling and sniggering outside the room which carried on for several minutes. Then it would stop and a few seconds later start up again. Eventually I got up to see what was going on and opened the door to find a large sign with a red arrow pointing to the keyhole. On to this Brian had written, for every passer by to see, 'You've heard Ray Moore's Saturday Night. Now listen to his Sunday Morning'. The sniggers and the scuffles were clearly from guests who had decided to take up Brian's thoughtful invitation.

Another memorable outing was a live Outside Broadcast (known as OB's in the trade) from Morecambe Pier. We were preceded on stage by a team of exotic topless dancers with tassels stuck to appropriate parts of their anatomy. Thank goodness this was radio! As the tassels bobbed and weaved in fetching contra-rotation some of them had a tendency to break free of their mooring and fly off in all directions. BBC producers are trained to be inventive under all circumstances and Steve Allen, who was in charge of us all, was no exception. He suggested that the girls used black Bostick to keep the tassels in place and thoughtfully provided a small tube of the stuff. Sticking them on was no problem. Getting them off was. And we have often wondered how the Morecambe showgirls ever managed to prise those tassels free. They must be getting quite moth eaten by now. And so must the tassels.

We also did a show one evening from a West End nightclub. Whether it was because the venue had been insufficiently re-searched beforehand or whether it was simply a case of 'every expense spared', I do not know to this day. But we arrived in a nightclub which was definitely at the seedier end of the range. It was a dance-till-dawn type of establishment but when we went on air at ten o'clock in the evening the place was deserted. Deserted, that is, except for a dozen 'hostesses' whose talents clearly encompassed more than merely serving drinks. We dreaded the news leaking out because it would have given the Sunday papers a field day – 'BBC Radio Show Live from a Brothel'.

Our shows were not confined to West End venues; indeed,

one of the benefits of the radio life has been the opportunity to travel up and down the country. For reasons which elude me now we had decided one year to stage a live OB from Kirriemuir in Scotland on New Year's Eve. The occasion got off to a dispiriting enough start as my producer, Steve Allen, and I pulled into Glasgow on a miserable, misty day. 'Now I know the meaning of McDuff', he said, foreshadowing the tone of the evening which was shortly to follow.

We did the show from Kirriemuir Village Hall which housed a bar stocking what seemed to be the produce of a thousand illicit Highland stills. The audience began to arrive in a staggering mass and quickly formed an impenetrable rugby scrum at the bar, pushing and shoving to get a drink. The local MC, togged up in the full Rob Roy kit, did his best to prise them away but without noticeable success. When the band arrived they showed the same fondness for a dram, and, after a while, it became clear that they were finding it increasingly difficult to stand up and play at the same time. The whole thing made for an eccentric listening experience; a drunken band, scraping and blowing away above the din of smashing glasses, dull thuds, as bodies hit the floor, and the bawling of the ancient Gaelic oaths. It threatened to become the first live riot on Radio 2.

The following New Year's Eve something rather more sedate was put forward. The BBC has what is known as a 'Radio Car', which is a kind of mobile studio, with a microphone relay back to Broadcasting House. This particular year someone suggested that the show should come from the Radio Car with me in the back giving a running commentary as it toured the West End. The music would be played in from the main studio in Broadcasting House leaving me to paint vivid word pictures of the excitement and bright lights as I cruised around. I set off at ten o'clock as the broadcast began and everything went well as we drove along Oxford Street and down Park Lane. I talked of the

[144]

revellers cavorting about as the last minutes of the Old Year ticked away; I painted pictures of the cheery celebrations I was driving past as group after group organised its own impromptu entertainment. But we were only about a quarter of an hour into the show when we hit a monumental traffic jam in Piccadilly and, unable to reverse, spent the next hour and a half in solid traffic which moved barely a couple of inches. My vivid word pictures became increasingly dull and repetitive, 'Well, here we are . . . still in Piccadilly . . . on my left is Old Bond Street leading up to Oxford Street . . . up ahead, Eros at Piccadilly Circus'. It was not the gripping stuff we had expected it to be. As midnight struck we were cruising morosely along the South Bank with me wittering on about the joys of Waterloo Station.

One of the best occasions of my early career was my very first trip abroad for Radio 2, involving me in a live OB with Sacha Distel in the glamorous surroundings of the Sporting d'Eté on the seafront at Monte Carlo. Among those whose lot it is to do interviews for a living, Sacha is well known as a generous and considerate interviewee. My friend Michael Aspel, with whom I have worked often over the years, told me recently, however, that Sacha's generosity was the unwitting cause of a rather tense moment he had on air.

Mike was hosting a show in the studio and interspersing the records with guest interviews. Sacha Distel was one of those due to appear. Unfortunately no-one seemed to have briefed the easy going Frenchman that the plan was to have a ten minute chat and then move on to another record and another guest. As a result, after Mike had drawn the interview to a close, Sacha stayed. A record followed and then Mike was forced to launch into another ten minutes of interviewing with the same guest, by this time taxing his interviewing technique quite severely. When Sacha continued to stay Mike found himself digging into every conceivable area of knowledge in order to keep the interview from fizzling out. Having exhausted all possible topics he could think of nothing new. In desperation he asked, after a marathon session, 'Well, Sacha, how are you keeping? You know, in yourself?'

Monte Carlo with Sacha Distel was my first taste of the high life. I soon became rather familiar with exotic away-days like these and have dear old Eurovision to thank for most of them.

I think back, for instance, to the year the Song Contest was coming from Jerusalem. The trip started in some splendour as we had dinner on the first night on the tenth floor of the Jerusalem Hilton overlooking the gleaming golden dome of the mosque as the sun was setting. The morning after I had a rather different impression of the city – and a more down to earth one at that. I was mooching about in the old town and popped into a dingy cave where they were peddling the beer and the grape. I ordered the beer, a vicious brew called Macabee, and sat there in the heat watching boys driving herds of sheep, goats, and donkeys up and down the alleyway outside. I was transfixed. Looking out on this passing tableau which had remained unchanged for two thousand years, I realised I was gazing at a scene in which Christ Himself could have taken part. And yet here was I, in this Holy City, to introduce such a glorious irrelevance as the Eurovision Song Contest. The contrast between the real world and our media world of make-believe could not have been stronger.

The delightful absurdity of these events was at its most acute, however, when the contest came from Paris and had Terry Wogan and me – co-voice-overs for the evening – reduced to incredulous giggles at the piffling nature of the whole thing.

At the rehearsals it appeared that the French had only just realised that day that they were supposed to be the hosts of this spectacle. There was constant argument as to who should do what and when, with eighteen different guys apparently in charge at any one time, and with eighteen different ideas of how best to proceed. It had the makings of a classic, first-rate shambles. At the dress rehearsal proper, things were going badly. Whole countries' delegations disappeared into thin air, the German song would be given a tumultuous introduction only to be followed by the appearance of a timid crooner representing Malta and all the while the score board consistently registered top marks for everyone. Suddenly the orchestra would strike up the intro to the Icelandic entry, while, standing on stage, was a bewildered Spanish tenor. The hapless individual hosting the show took on the air of a broken man.

At a break in rehearsal I popped down to the loo, only to find host and director slugging it out with bare fists as a line of gents attending to their own business peered over their shoulders to watch proceedings. No Eurovision Song Contest had evoked such passion before. Sadly for Terry and me the live transmission that night went remarkably smoothly.

But it was the Contest from Dublin which, for sheer eccentricity, I remember with most affection. It was the year of the Hunger Strikes and the local Garda obviously felt the British contingent were particularly at risk – whether for our policy in Northern Ireland or for the quality of our song I cannot recall. Either way, we all had armed guards night and day and were whisked by coach to rehearsals, to the accompaniment of screaming motorcycle outriders and helicopters whirring overhead. It seemed a little excessive.

As we were to be in Dublin for four days, Alma decided to come over with me to make a short holiday of it. From the brochure the hotel we were staying in looked delightful. 'Standing in five acres of beautiful gardens', it cooed. On our first day Alma decided on a tour of these five acres of beautiful gardens to enjoy them to the full. We did ten laps of the hotel but found no hint of a garden, only a miserable patch of grass alongside the car park. We enquired at the desk as to the whereabouts of these Elysian five acres. 'Ah, well, you see, sir', came the reply, 'The hotel is built *in* the five acres all around us, the hotel stands *in* the five acres'.

One day, I was taken on a conducted tour of the city. As we reached the top of O'Connell Street I noticed a lovely old building with stained glass windows, obviously some sort of ecclesiastical establishment. 'A seminary? A monastery?' I enquired. 'Yes, indeed', he replied, 'and you don't want to be bothering with that. It's a hot bed of celibacy in there!'

Just down the road from the hotel was the railway station at the side of which was one of those small, miserable railway sheds. This was a particularly rotting affair with cobwebbed windows and holes in the roof – for all the world like Dad's old garden shed in Waterloo. On the side wall of this shack, however, was one of those wrought iron plaques with elaborately embossed lettering. 'THESE PREMISES', it ran, 'ARE NOT THE PROPERTY OF THE DUKE OF CONNAUGHT'. I found it baffling that His Grace, the Duke, should find time to take his mind off weighty affairs of state to be bothered about this mouldy shed. And why should he be so concerned to dissociate himself from ownership? Perhaps the place harboured a dark family secret which only this wrought iron disclaimer could disguise. In the gloomy watches of the night this mystery bothers me still.

[9]

If whimsical eccentricity was my trademark then two other men hold title deeds to the patent.

For a long time Colin Berry preceded me on the air, in the way that I was to precede Wogan. The end result of this was that over many years we saw each other five days a week and grew to be good friends. My earliest recollection of Colin dates back in 1968 when he was a young record plugger who regularly turned up at The George at lunchtime wearing a baggy pink suit, a very daring number even for those liberated times. The record plugger's art lay in his ability to push new releases enthusiastically in the direction of disc-jockeys and producers, in the hope that the black vinyl would get an airing over the radio. The job demanded reserves of physical energy, a pool of mental agility, a thick skin and the knack of getting on with people however trying the circumstances. In every department Colin qualified with distinction. Over the years since then, the ostentatious suit has fallen away but the personal qualities remain, qualities put severely to the test on holidays and week-ends which Alma and I spent with him.

On one excursion to the South coast it was suggested we try a local fish restaurant named 'The Mad Chef'. We decided to test it out and, as it was not licensed, trooped in laden with carrier bags full of wine which clanked as we walked. The chef himself greeted us with a flourish, making great play of despatching waiters, solicitously to take our coats. He himself looked rather like Salvador Dali with a long thin moustache and wild eyes. We sensed an interesting evening ahead.

We consulted the menu which boasted every conceivable fishy dish known to man and, after long deliberation, I chose the turbot, Alma, the plaice and Colin, the Dover sole. Before tackling this spread I nipped downstairs to the loo and noticed, next door, a large room containing a king-sized double bed on which was piled layer upon layer of coats, scarves and hats – one of them I succeeded in identifying as Alma's. So here was the 'cloakroom'. After meticulously greeting his guests the Mad Chef was, once out of sight, apparently flinging their clothes onto a random heap.

Eventually the food arrived and each of us was presented with a large bowl of fish stew with mussels, prawns and squid bobbing up and down in a fiery red sauce. It looked tasty enough but was not what we had ordered. We called over the chef and pointed out the error. He did not seem at all concerned and merely replied, as if the explanation sufficed, 'Ah, well, you see, sir, I'm mad. Mad, don't you know, mad. So what do you expect?'

For me no two weeks would be the same and the scope of my professional life has probably never been as wide. At the BBC we were hired simply as 'announcers' which meant presiding over anything from concerts for light entertainment to World Service newsreading at Bush House, the home of the Corporation's External Services.

It was during this period that I presented a very popular little show on Sunday mornings. It was called 'Banners and Bonnets' and was a twenty minute programme of Salvation Army music. It had a loyal following among Christian believers and non-believers alike. It was thanks to this programme that I met a man who, at critical points in my life, seems to have been on hand to help me out. His name is Harry Read, then a junior officer in the Army, whose job it was to come onto the programme half way through and give a potted sermon. This was a model of concision and down-to-earth Christianity.

There was nothing over-pious about this little Geordie man but he exuded a kind of 'ordinary' saintliness. He was, and is, a man who seemed to radiate goodness while steadfastly avoiding any trace of the 'goody-goody'. His simple, profound faith and his no-nonsense approach won him a devoted following and I, too, came under his influence.

The funny thing was that when Harry left for Canada much later on, by now promoted to quite senior rank, we never lost contact. Our letters seemed miraculously to cross in the post. For months I might not write, only to find that suddenly, after eventually sending off a letter to him, one of his letters would arrive on our doormat the next day.

The demise of 'Banners and Bonnets' was not the only change at Broadcasting House. Once Radios 1, 2, 3 and 4 had been created the need to 'specialise' was the curse that fell on all the announcers who were now forced to choose between the networks. I opted for Radio 2 and found that, at a stroke, there were no more newsreading shifts and no more concerts. I found the new system rather restricting after all the work I had done before so in 1973, at the comparatively late age of thirty-one, I took a risk and went freelance – selling my services as a broadcaster to whoever could use me.

It was, I suppose, rather arrogant of me to think I could survive in London without one stable employer but it was a move prompted, in part, by pragmatism. But I had been blessed with a good voice and it seemed a betrayal not to use it to the full.

Thus began a delightfully eclectic period of professional life. TV trailers and voice-overs for advertisements; commentary on science programmes like 'Horizon' and 'Q.E.D.'; introductions at 'The Ideal Home Exhibition' or 'The Variety Club Awards'; everything from the high-brow to the low, including promotional videos about paint and drains.

I was always keen to do more serious documentaries but the powers in charge seemed to think I had a 'light entertainment' voice so I got rather stuck in that area but enjoyed it all the same. On Miss World for instance, I loved the garishness of the occasion and the glamour of the showbiz environment. Of course, I knew it was false and hollow but if you accepted it as such and did not fall for the make-believe it was a very pleasant world in which to work. I would never have watched Miss World at home but it gave me a real kick to be introducing it live. Even though he is hidden away in a box somewhere, the guy who has to say, 'Tonight, live from London . . .' has got one of the most exciting jobs around. It's egomania running wild.

I suppose that feeling came to a head when I was booked to do the voice over for the Laurence Olivier Awards on BBC2, at which His Royal Highness, Prince Edward was guest. I could hear on my earpiece the producer shouting out, 'For God's sake don't let HRH appear in the Royal Box until Ray gives him the say-so!' It is a source of abiding amusement that Prince Edward had to hang around in the wings picking his nose until some Scouser backstage gave him the go-ahead.

The freelance work was also an opportunity to get a worm's eye view of all sorts of entertainment, warts and all. An audience would see the glitter and the seemingly effortless finished product; the presenters would see how it *really* was. We used to call it the 'swan effect', so termed because of the beguiling impression a swan can project. All may be stately and calm on the surface, but, underneath, his flippers are pedalling like mad.

This was, for some reason, particularly true of the many dance competitions I hosted. People often remark that the Miss World competitions must be tense and catty affairs but let me tell them, they were sweet reason in comparison to the World Dancing finals. The dancers – total professionals, it has to be said – were inordinately conscious of their own dignity, and so completely lacking in any sense of humour that it was often a rather prickly occasion. You were allowed no licence to invent or embellish. Whatever announcement or intro. you made had to be a flat-footed statement of the obvious. 'Now, couple number 16, John Smith and Jane Jones' was the absolute limit of creative imagination allowed. Once, by way of injecting a measure of humour into the proceedings I made some vaguely witty and totally innocuous remark only to be buttonholed after the show by a couple who poked their fingers in my chest and said, 'Look here, you seem to think this is some kind of entertainment!'

Being backstage like this gave me a privileged glimpse of those moments that an audience never sees. One of these was at a Sunday afternoon rehearsal at the London Palladium for the Royal Variety Performance. I was there preparing my an-nouncements while on stage the ventriloquist Roger de Courcy and his 'partner' Nooky Bear were on stage going through their routine. At the back of the auditorium sat the glowering figure of Robert Nesbitt, the great impresario and producer. This man, venerated across the entire span of the entertainment business, looked on unamused and clearly in a foul temper. After a few moments he rose from his seat, stormed towards the stage and tore Roger de Courcy off more than a couple of strips in front of the whole cast who had suddenly fallen silent. 'The material's dull', he boomed, 'the act's not coming across. The whole thing's wrong'. Roger de Courcy, by now extremely embar-rassed, muttered his apologies and said, yes, he would tighten up the act for the big night. Then Robert Nesbitt strode back to his seat. As he was halfway back a voice from the stage called out, 'But wait a minute, Nesbitt, what do you know about this?' You could have heard a pin drop. The great man swivelled round and glared at the person who had dared to speak to him in this way. It was the bear. 'Just bugger off, Bob', it continued, 'and leave me and Rog. to look after this ourselves'. Meanwhile, with mock concern, Roger de Courcy tried to clamp a hand on Nooky Bear's mouth as he told him not to be so rude in front of all these people.

Not everyone I met was pacified as easily. I recall inadvertently upsetting Englebert Humperdinck on a show in which he was providing the cabaret and I, the introductory announcements. He turned up wearing a very expensive, tailored jacket, made out of chamois leather, an elaborate outfit which seemed to me to be the sartorial equivalent of my denim safari suit of distant memory. As he walked by I casually said, 'At least you'll never be unemployed'.

'What do you mean?' he asked blankly.

'Well, if the singing doesn't work out, you can always get a window cleaning round.'

But it was my radio work which was still the mainspring of my professional life. And here let me describe the architect of this anarchic enterprise, my producer for many years, Dennis O'Keeffe.

Dennis, a round faced, jolly man with a boyish enthusiasm for the impossible and the half-baked, is the proverbial 'legend in his own lunchtime', a one time professional drummer with a musician's wicked sense of fun. We were constantly having 'planning meetings' to cook up ever more ridiculous ideas for outside broadcasts, and the fact that these 'planning meetings' invariably took place in the congested corners of The Northumberland Arms led to some ridiculous ideas indeed.

A Good Friday morning OB from Norwich was one I recall with some bewilderment. The town was deserted, the shops shut, the traffic silent. The odd vicar scurried from service to service and we, goodness knows how, were left to fill two hours of air time.

At this time, one has to remember that John Dunn seemed constantly to be jetting off to Hong Kong, Gloria Hunniford to Florida and Brian Matthew to New York. If we could not equal the competition in exotic locations, Dennis and I thought we should attempt celebrity at the opposite extreme. Accordingly, one Bank Holiday Monday, our OB crew turned up in Deptford, South East London, which is a long way from being Mayfair and resembles, on the surface of things, at least, an archetype of inner city decay. But Deptford High Street, normally thick with a milling throng of humanity on week-days, had an air of desolation on Bank Holiday. We agreed it was a most peculiar venue for a broadcast but salvaged the day, in the end, by broadcasting an equally peculiar, boozy knees-up in the Trafalgar Tavern with Chas and Dave and Wendy Richard. An odd event at eleven-thirty on a Monday morning by any standards.

Another brainwave was to travel further North for our broadcasts. And where more obvious than Liverpool? We arrived on Christmas Eve with the city swathed in a Scouse pea-souper. Most people had either gone to families for the holiday or were busy tearing about the streets, too intent on last minute shopping to spare a thought for the Prodigal Son, home to do a programme. In the end we were reduced to cruising the streets at a snail's pace in the Radio Car negotiating the dense traffic and the fog. Eventually we turned up at the Roman Catholic Cathedral, known locally as the Pope's Wigwam. At least we assumed it was the Roman Catholic Cathedral because although we could hear the bells, we could not actually see the church. I spent most of the two hours giving vivid descriptions of things which, through the gloom, I could not see.

The OB did have the advantage of allowing me a few days at

[155]

home with the family, a luxury which the growing pressure of work sometimes made difficult. I tried to get back as often as I could because Dad was suffering from heart trouble and I felt an instinctive urge to spend as much as possible of what were clearly to be his last couple of years with him and Mum. In the last four years of his life we became very close and we finally made our peace long before he died. He was very proud of me.

We used to talk about his absence a lot. For once this painful period was no longer out of bounds and we used to tell each other of the deep emotions that were racking us both at the time. We would be close to tears as he told of his regret at leaving us all, and at treating Mum so badly. I, too, explained the contradictory emotions that I felt, both when he left and when he returned.

At other times, though, he would regale me with hysterically funny stories about the things he had got up to in drink. He would look back on those tales as if they had happened to someone else, which, in a way, I suppose, they had, and he would laugh until I thought he would explode. I remember him quaking with laughter during one of the last conversations I ever had with him. By now a series of strokes had debilitated him and it broke his heart that he had to go to the pub in a cab. At the end of one conversation, though, he became tearful as he asked me to promise that, when the end, which he knew was not far off, finally came, I would take him home to be buried on the Isle of Man.

Dad died, aged seventy-three, in March 1980. It was a time which coincided with another family trauma and I, caught between the two, was pulled in two separate directions.

Alma had been suffering for some time from problems in the area known by my mother as 'down below'. Eventually it was suggested that a hysterectomy should be performed. The timing could not have been more unfortunate. Within a week of her returning home to convalesce, news that my father had died reached us.

In the end I resolved this terrible dilemma in the only way I thought right. I went up to Liverpool to see to the funeral arrangements and, probably unaware of the real extent of Alma's psychological state, promised to phone twice a day to keep as close to her as I could. I had not bargained for the intense emotional swings to which she was going to be subjected after the operation. One moment I would phone and it would be, 'Darling, please don't leave me. I love you so much', the next it would be, 'You heartless so-and-so, you don't love me at all. If you did you'd be down here with me while I'm in agony'.

Meanwhile I was having to contend with problems enough in Liverpool. A normal funeral is bad enough but in addition to attending to pensions and insurance policies, having to export a body, which is what it amounted to, was taking a heavy toll. I had to book the boat and organise the grave on the Isle of Man, while telephoning Alma to find her in floods of tears, begging me to come back straight away. The aftermath, too, was traumatic in the extreme and I covered it in the best way I knew how; by going back to work on the following Monday and throwing myself into it with even greater vigour.

A new challenge was, by now, awaiting me as I had just taken up tenure of the early morning show on Radio 2, set to run from 5.30am until 7.30am, in preference to a late evening programme which I felt had a much smaller following.

It involved little preparation as such, other than a detailed scrutiny of the letters that came in. I would gauge the mood of the letters, note the more unusual ones and then, with no more than a couple of handwritten notes to keep me going, launch into two hours of free flight. I would make sure that take off and landing were executed well – but the space between would be a kind of joint adventure with presenter and listener sharing an indefinable complicity.

My theory, if I ever had one, was that this show, broadcast at such a crazy time could only be successful if it were based on one assumption: that nobody in his or her right mind would *choose* to be up at such an awful hour. If we both had to be awake so early, I thought, let's agree one thing: that it's you and me against the world. I determined to be cheerful but in a grumpy sort of way, with none of the enforced jollity so beloved of Radio 4. My message was, 'If you think it's fun being up at 5.30, you're fooling yourself. Both you and I know that it isn't the best thing in the world to be up before even the cat has come home. So let's agree, at least, on that and try and make the best of things'.

As a by-product of this show I was also beginning to develop a rapport with the man who took over the airwaves after me; Terry Wogan. That relationship became a strange, good humoured double act which I treasure today as one of the unpredictable perks of this glorious business.

But first, after the trauma of Dad's death and Alma's operation, Alma and I needed a holiday and so in the summer of '81 we set off for Corfu. Our good friend Colin Berry had married, inappropriately enough on Independence Day, and had invited the two of us to go on honeymoon with him and his wife Sandra. It seemed a bizarre idea at first but, given that the four of us were far from strangers, it began to look quite logical. The episode took on a rather less rosy dimension when, after five days away, I became semi-housebound thanks to a boating accident. The four of us must have created a strange picture: Colin and Sandra mooning about deliriously happy and me sitting morosely by the pool – Alma, meanwhile wondering why she should ever have got involved with the entire enterprise in the first place. What had happened was this.

The boat we had hired to take us round the coast was pulling into a beautiful deserted bay and, as it neared the shore, I leapt out, Captain Cook-like, to mark landfall. Sadly for me my heel came into painful contact with a sharp rock and within minutes my foot had swollen so alarmingly that I had to be manhandled back into the boat. By the time we reached our hotel the foot, too painful to stand on, had turned a worrying shade of black. For some obscure reason no doctor could be summoned until the next day, so I settled down to an excruciating night during which my foot began to assume the proportion of a weather balloon.

The medic, when he finally arrived, recommended an X-ray in Corfu Town and gave us the address of a second doctor whose surgery was up three flights of stairs above an evil smelling souk. By now it was midday and, with the temperature in the high nineties, I crawled up the staircase on all threes (the fourth being practically useless). After what seemed like an eternity I was helped in to see the doctor, a heavy lidded, George Coulouris type, surrounded by the oddest selection of iron-mongery I had ever seen. This turned out to be his X-ray kit and was quite obviously one of Madame Curie's early prototypes. I refused to subject myself to this apparently lethal radioactive meccano set, a refusal which sent the doctor into a towering rage. After he had calmed down I casually enquired about the possibility of borrowing a pair of crutches. This remark triggered such a torrent of derisory laughter that for a moment I thought I had asked for a sedan chair and four native bearers. Eventually a wooden broom handle with a wad of cloth appeared. I decided to wait until I returned to London for treatment so, as an interim measure, he bound the foot in a porridge bandage weighing half a ton and so rendered me less mobile than I had been when I arrived.

Back at the hotel the problems of mobility were increased. The hotel itself was a modern affair, all glass and marble, and every morning a team of swarthy, middle aged women would appear to polish the floors with an obsessive zeal. As the day progressed these floors would then be liberally covered in water and suntan oil from the constant parade of bare feet to and from the pool. By the end of the day it was unsafe to cross the main lobby without snow shoes. That night, as Alma and I were hobbling across to dinner, my makeshift crutch landed on a particularly shiny patch and shot from under me. Like a poor man's Long John Silver on the skids I hit the marble with a loud crash and the bad foot banged heavily against the wall causing a searing stab of pain to tear up my leg. By now the porridge bandage was almost visibly vibrating and giving off an offensive pong into the bargain. I was convinced gangrene was the next logical development.

One of the holiday makers at the hotel was a lugubrious Scottish doctor who would have made Jeremiah seem like the life and soul of the party. He gave me an instant opinion. I should be put in plaster from hip to toe for a minimum of six months after which time I would probably never walk again, certainly not on rough ground. Stairs would be a permanent problem and in later life I would suffer from arthritis. I walked into dinner enormously relieved. So it wasn't too bad after all!

Clearly, in Corfu, illness was an irritating inconvenience. If you did fall sick you were expected to retire to your room, curl up in a corner and die quietly without disturbing the peace and quiet of the island. Blank stares of disbelief greeted my request for a wheelchair but after a few days an antediluvian wickerwork commode appeared and I took up residence in it looking like Queen Victoria on the throne. Many people sympathised with me about the foot but thought it a particularly cruel twist of fate to be stricken with incontinence as well. This was the Year of the Disabled and so I was treated to a parade of wags telling me I was supposed to help them not join them.

Inundated with messages of good-will

Alma and I take a walk on the heath

With London in the background

Proud parents and grandmother

Above: With Management.
Right: While taking a break to
write the book. Sussex, March
1988

February 1988 as Alma and I look to the future

Eventually we returned home where the leg was put in plaster up to the knee and I was furnished with a pair of lightweight crutches on which I hobbled for the next four months. During this time I made two surprising discoveries; that you need two legs even to shave yourself, and that the crutches react strangely with alcohol. After a bottle of wine it felt as if the crutches had turned into rubber.

I mention my geriatric state of mobility at some length for one reason. To paint a picture of the shambles I was in when Dennis, my producer, and I decided to be more ambitious in our choice of 'away days' and to plan a trip to America. Dennis had run into a music publisher who reckoned he was Tom Jones' 'man' in London. He suggested we record an interview with Tom, illustrate it with his hit records, and make a one hour radio special. The message came back that Tom would be happy to record the interview in Vancouver where he was recording some TV shows. We could not justify the expense to the BBC without including a second artist in our round trip so, after some negotiation, we secured the co-operation of the Carpenters who said they would be delighted to be interviewed in Hollywood. This was more like it, a considerable improvement on Deptford High Street, and a glittering occasion marred only by my crutches and shambling gait.

After numerous changes of plane and thirty hours without sleep we eventually arrived in Vancouver. Tom Jones' manager arranged the interview for three in the afternoon and, after what seemed an interminable wait, we were finally ushered into the presence of the great man at six thirty that evening. Tom, casual in dressing gown, had just got up and was tucking into scrambled egg. His routine involved taping the television shows at eleven at night, dancing away until dawn, and then sleeping throughout the day, a peculiar lifestyle which accounted for his somewhat bleary appearance.

After our interview, which went very well, I asked him if I could buy him a drink. He declined at first, saying he never touched a drop before the show, but after a moment's reflection decided on a bottle of champagne. Obviously he considered it to be no more potent than sarsparilla. It cost me forty-nine quid.

Dennis and I left him to his topsy turvy life and went for dinner to an adjacent hotel where we sat in the revolving restaurant watching Vancouver pass by below us. I put my cigarettes on the window sill and when I came to look for them they were half way round the room. I asked one of the waiters where the Gents was and he said, 'It's either to the left or the right, but if you hang on here it'll come round to you in a minute'.

After a day trip to Vancouver Island where they had a museum of antiquities boasting exhibits dating as far back as 1912, we left on a flight for Los Angeles on a clapped out aircraft which looked as if it had been assembled from a kit in a junk yard. I have a friend who has a phobia about flying at the best of times (indeed he was so relieved after one journey that he tipped the pilot of a scheduled European airline a tenner) and I could not help wondering what he would have made of this ramshackle jet which looked as if it were taking part in a pre-war air display. After lurches and jolts even the concrete brutalism of LA Airport seemed a relief.

We were met at the airport by an enormous limousine provided by the Carpenters' Record Company and taken to the Sportsman's Lodge in Hollywood, just off Coldwater Canyon. It was an odd place with all the rooms facing onto a swimming pool where guests lounged around receiving what I am sure were fake messages on the tannoy.

'Twentieth Century Fox calling Mamie Hogwash.'

'The Walt Disney Corporation calling Milton Epstein Junior.'

It seemed to be an opportunity rich in comic potential so one day, unable to resist the temptation, I arranged for my own message:

'Mr Sinatra calling Mr O'Keeffe from the BBC.'

Dennis had to return to the bar to steady his nerves before taking the dud call.

The Carpenters had by now agreed to see us on Sunday and Dennis, good Catholic that he is, suggested we precede the great event by going to church in the morning. We found a large, Spanish style church in the heart of Hollywood and sat sheepishly at the back. At one point in the service, our prayers were asked for a local parishioner. There then followed a roll-call of ancient Hollywood luminaries after which, at the end of the service, the priest gave the Benediction, 'May the peace of God be in your hearts and minds, today and forever more. Amen. Have a nice day, now.'

As we got to the studios where the interview had been arranged, we were introduced to Herb Alpert. 'Hi, Ray', he said as if we were long lost friends, 'Great to know ya.' Not so familiar with such instant cordiality I felt rather embarrassed to hear myself say, 'Hi, Herb, great to know ya, too.'

He asked what sort of station Radio 2 was – Heavy Metal perhaps? – and seemed nonplussed when I told him it was more Dralon Velvet than Hard Rock.

The Carpenters were everything I had hoped for and more. Richard, all scrubbed and squeaky clean with the fresh-faced College boy look about him and Karen so beautiful with haunted eyes more bewitching in life than on any television screen. She had a fragile vulnerability about her which made her even more attractive. Tragically her death was only months away.

Sitting there chatting on that sunny Sunday afternoon in Hollywood was one of the happiest and most relaxed times of my life. During the interview Karen wanted to illustrate some particular point about their career together and she started singing, 'Long ago and oh so far away I fell in love with you before the second show . . .'

I think I had fallen in love with her myself. At the end of the recording which they seemed to enjoy as much as we did the two of them climbed into one of those John De Lorean cars and sped off into the setting sun.

I reached for my aluminium crutches and hobbled off into the same sunset with Dennis by my side looking for a bar.

The one we settled on was 'The Cock and Bull' which was clearly designed to be a replica of a genuine English pub and had the sort of half-timbered artificiality which made it evident that the designer had never been near the real thing at all. It was full of people who had nearly been famous. The pianist had once appeared in a B movie with two stars I had never heard of. The barman used to live next door to a chap who had a bit part in 'Casablanca' and the waitress had a son who used to go to school with the bass guitarist in Toto. 'All the stars who never were are parking cars and pumping gas'.

Back in Britain I returned to the familiar rhythm of the early morning show and found that my brush with Hollywood had in no way overshadowed the plain thrill of presenting what was, by comparison, a pretty unglamorous product. I still loved the buzz of being on air. As a newsreader some twelve years earlier I had relished that egocentric feeling. Delivering the 8am news bulletin was a great, crunchy experience and you just bit it. I thought to myself, 'They may switch off at ten past eight but, by God, they're going to listen to me for ten minutes first'. The early show was a rather different experience with scope for developing a genuine relationship with listeners. In some strange way I got back from them what I was giving out. It was a two way traffic. Over the years I established an emotional attachment to listeners who were not 'listeners' at all. They were individuals in their own right. That is why I could never understand presenters who began with 'Good morning, everyone'. There is not an 'everyone' out there. There is just you. There may be three million listening in homes and cars but for the time I was on the air I was talking to them one at a time.

In the end I developed a sort of sixth sense which enabled me to know how listeners were reacting to things I did. With children, for example, I knew from their letters what made them laugh and would know instinctively if they were listening to my reply on the radio. There was no room for pretence at that time of the morning and I knew if I put on a cheery morning act people would see through it in an instant. Many of the listeners wrote in to say how they built their day around the morning show and complained that, if I went on holiday, it would disorientate them. And that was all part of the joy. They were reading me and my moods just as I was gauging theirs. I would get a hundred or more letters a day – many of them from regulars who felt free to react in any way they liked, to complain, to praise, to suggest or, merely, to share something. And I was constantly being showered with gifts.

At Christmas time I once casually mentioned a phrase of my mother's, 'I'm going to get everybody hankies this year. You can never get enough hankies'. And, of course, the studio was inundated with them. Gifts of wedding cake, and birthday cake were regularly appearing along with homemade buns, photographs of listeners in the garden, cigarettes, cigars or perfume brought back for me from a holiday they had been on. And the feelings which prompted such generosity were genuine, as if they felt they knew me well enough to offer such presents as one member of a family to another. It was a relationship I loved. These were more than just 'fan letters'.

On occasions money would arrive with a note attached, 'Enjoyed the show. Here's a fiver. Have a drink on me, Ray'.

Obviously I could not accept the money because of the BBC's strict code on things like that, so I would write back to explain and to thank them for the gesture. Such a letter was once taken by one old lady as the height of rudeness and ingratitude. Out of the goodness of her heart she had sent me some money for a Christmas drink. I wrote back to explain the restrictions on this kind of thing, thanked her warmly and wished her every happiness for the festive season. That was not the end of it.

Some days later I got a second letter from her containing a torrent of abuse. Out of pure generosity in the season of goodwill, she said, she had sent me a gift and I had just flung it back in her face! At least it proved that people felt they could treat me as part of the family – praising me one minute and ticking me off the next. People coming on to the show to take over from me for a couple of weeks while I was on holiday told me they felt as though they were intruding into an intimate relationship.

The letters expressed that intimacy, too. After a while on air I was almost talking in code, with a whole series of 'in' jokes and shared experiences that brought us all that much closer. The letters I received reflected this and were written in the same sort of code which only I would be able to understand. Even Alma at times had to admit she could not decipher the code and was at a loss to understand what it was a listener was getting at.

They would write in in that ironic, very 'British' way. It might begin with a snatch of well-aimed abuse, complaining about the drivel I was talking and assuring me that letters to the Director General were being planned; that my show was pure rubbish which should not be allowed on the air five days a week and so on. At the end, almost as an afterthought, they would write, 'By the way, my mother's eighty on Friday. You couldn't give her a mention, could you?'

There was never any rigid plan to these shows. Dennis would preselect all the music, then I would plan the mechanics of it – which meant getting into the Greenwich pips cleanly, for example, and introducing the newsreader properly. But after that it varied from day to day. Perhaps the news would overrun or, in winter, there would be a motoring flash or an extra sports report – no two days were the same. And, of course, the mail was unpredictable. A particularly good letter, incorporated into the programme at the right time, would dictate the direction of a whole new strand of lunacy the following week, as listeners pursued a theme.

They were a very varied crowd – people who had just come off the night shift, or were setting off for the early one, nurses, farmers, the elderly who had risen early, unable to sleep, unemployed people and, later in the show, kids going off to school. There was another strain of letter I received from time to time and these I treasure above all; the letters, sometimes unsigned, from people who had been pulled back from the brink by something I had said, from people on the very edge of suicide who maintained that they, thanks to me, had decided to give life another try after all, from people who thanked me for hauling them out of some pit of depression, or from people who were simply relieved to hear me sounding as if I understood something of the heartache they were experiencing at that defenceless time in the still of the morning.

When the Pearly Gates do finally heave into view I might just manage to point to this small achievement, by way of getting in credit with the Almighty, before He reaches His final judgement and hands me the paperwork to sign.

Another key listener to all this, of course, would be Terry Wogan, who, by now, would be driving in, ready to take over at 7.30. We went in for a sort of verbal tennis at the changeover and each reacted to what the other had said the day before. This was liberally sprinkled with insults which could only work if we were in sympathy with one another. You cannot be insulting to somebody whom you do not like and whose work you do not appreciate – if you are, people might end up believing you. The relationship was a very rich and enduring one.

It was also enlivened by the unexpected. Normally Terry would not be in the studio much before 7.25. He would take his hat off, sit down and just get on with the show. We had an arrangement that if anybody is ever late the person already in the seat carries on until the other arrives.

One morning, however, there was no sign of Terry at 7.30. I carried on for five or ten minutes and then he showed up, obviously in a furious temper. When he got himself together and a record was playing he told me what had happened. Apparently, on the drive in somebody had been too close on his tail and when the cars braked the chap behind had skidded into Terry's Rolls, causing, as you could imagine, a lot of damage. So not only was he annoyed about being late he was also preoccupied with having to sort out the repairs. He and the driver exchanged addresses to Terry's obvious annoyance because the other man was to blame. As he was climbing back into the Rolls, the man came running up, forced Terry to wind down the window and said, 'By the way, Tel, you couldn't play us a record when you get in, could you?'

On many occasions, I have been quite amazed at how insulting some people can be because they think you are public property. They assume you have no sensitivity at all as they crowd around for autographs. I was with Terry once at a 'Come Dancing' show and was staggered by some of the reactions. They would come up and say things like, 'I can't bear you for one moment and I never listen to your show but would you sign this, it's for my sister'. No-one seemed to think that some of the things they said might be hurtful. And in a sense, the bigger you were, the

[168]

ruder they felt they could be. I am a low key, workaday sort of person so I did not get too much of that reaction but somebody like Terry came in for his share of it.

I remember once inadvertently hurting him myself – something which saddened me and made me realise what pressures real stardom puts on a public figure. For some weeks Terry had been referring on his show to the soap opera 'Dallas' so I, in a well intentioned and tongue-in-cheek way, referred to that fact on mine. 'Isn't it a shame about Terry?' I said in an ironic tone. 'Having to stay at home all night watching TV. Obviously the poor guy never gets out to the theatre or for a meal and has to sit in every evening and watch Dallas'. I expected to hear no more about it but he came into the studio looking hurt and offended. He said, 'Look, Ray, you know there are only about three or four restaurants in this country where we can eat without being pestered. So we've got to stay in to protect our privacy and keep a bit of sanity'. I explained it was just a gag but I felt awful about the whole thing.

Our relationship lasted, I think, because we adopted two different roles. I played the low-life to Terry's high-life. Because I don't drive Terry used to tease me for not having a car and having to trudge through the snow to get from home to work. I, in return, could talk about him being the cosmic megastar being chauffeured everywhere he chose. The arrangement worked very well and each of us could capitalise on an imagined trait in the other and let our fantasies weave extraordinary fictions around it. This was how Alma began to be brought in on the act. Terry would make great play of how Alma had to do all the shopping on foot because I was too mean to buy a car. It was thanks to Terry that the notion of 'Big Alma' made it on air – I was depicted as being under her thumb, ready to get eight bells knocked out of me if I was late, which, once again, if he thought it was true, he would never have said. It was a great, good-humoured fantasy which added colour to both our shows.

In fact the reality could not have been further removed from the fiction. Over the years Alma has had to cope with all sorts of strange ways of mine and has done so without a moan. Well, without too many moans, shall we say?

Keeping strange hours imposed its own disciplines. Along with all the associated problems: funny eating habits, bad temper, the odd drink too many. And in all of it Alma has been wonderful, offering much more support than I ever deserved. There were times when, having set out at three in the morning, I would not be home from work until ten or eleven at night. And when I did get in I was so tired that all I could do was fall into bed without having the strength to stay up and chat. Many weeks we hardly saw each other but she was always there cheerful and tolerant of what, at times, was a very selfish routine.

The morning shows could wreak havoc on a social life. Once we invited some friends round for dinner. They arrived about eight and after what seemed like hours I remember feeling totally defeated by tiredness and saying, 'Well, I think you'd better go now, I'm off to bed'. It was ten past nine. Then there was the time we had invited Alma's son, David, and his wife to spend the weekend with us. They were due to arrive at Friday teatime and I had booked a table at one of our favourite restaurants. After a spectacularly busy week, with very little sleep, I got home on Friday by mid-afternoon and decided I would have an hour's snooze to refresh myself for the evening ahead. The next thing I remembered was waking up at 9am the following morning, having resisted all attempts to rouse me from this catatonic slumber.

Getting up so early can have other unpredictable side effects – like not really knowing whether, at that time, I was awake or asleep. I have always been a heavy sleeper, given to vivid dreams and occasional sleepwalking. I remember one morning getting up and deciding to flush my socks down the loo. And in those dead hours before dawn I often used to crawl out of bed in my usual comatose state and climb into the wardrobe looking for the toilet: I could never understand why someone had put all those coats, and suits, and shirts in the bathroom. 'I hope you're not *doing* anything in there, Ray', Alma would say.

Alma always seems to have the right, understated phrase for every occasion. If I were going out to lunch: 'Don't you let me down and start having fun'; or a reception: 'You don't *have* to drink, you know'; or a film: 'You've just had a whole pint of beer, you can't still be thirsty'; or any other time: 'It's like having a child in the house'. Throughout it all Alma has endured my anti-social eccentricities with quiet resignation.

When the pressure has got too much we have had to wrench ourselves away from the daily routine and get a holiday. Often this has meant getting as far away from London as possible. One memorable holiday took us to Toronto in 1984. I seem to remember this transatlantic Odyssey beginning with another of her gnomic remarks, 'I'm not going anywhere with you until you get some decent underpants!' This lament was flung at me daily for weeks before the trip. I began to conjure up a picture of us arriving at Toronto airport, and checking through passport control only to have the customs man saying, 'Right, let's see your underpants'. There we would stay if he did not consider my underpants decent enough. The remark was on a par with another of Alma's favourites, 'What will people think of me if you go out dressed like that?' Quite how people could form a balanced opinion of Alma based on the state of my trousers, I could never fathom.

It was on our Toronto trip that we decided to visit the Niagara Falls. It was pouring with rain and a thick mist hung everywhere. We stood around for an hour or so listening to the whooshing of water but never actually managed to see the cascade. It gave a whole new meaning to the line in the song, 'We'll go again to Niagara. This time we'll look at the Falls'.

While we were there I decided to look up my friend and guardian angel, Harry Read, the Salvation Army officer who had so impressed me all those years before. A very strange thing occurred. I telephoned him out of the blue one morning to see if we might meet up for lunch. He picked up the phone and said, yes, of course, come over. Nothing strange in that. But there was; because, when we met, Harry told me that he had been posted to Australia and that that day was his very last in Canada. In fact he had actually sold his house that day and was just paying it a final five minute call, to check all was OK, when the phone rang. And it was me.

Back home the usual routine beckoned. Early morning radio and the odd TV appearance on a special show. On these I was, more often than not, out of vision or, if not, usually asked to play understudy to Michael Aspel or Terry Wogan. I was quite frequently asked if I ever resented playing the monkey to someone else's organ grinder. The answer was always an emphatic 'no'. Terry, Mike and I (or anybody else for that matter) are three different people, playing three different roles, with three different sorts of strength. It's impossible to say, on radio, for example, that Brian Redhead is better than Jimmy Young, or that Mike Read is not as good as Robin Day. All are different.

On our radio shows people might suggest I was a sort of warm up man for the main event but that was to mistake the idea behind Terry's show and mine. There was some overlap, of course, but by and large we had our separate audiences and both of us made those differences our individual strengths. Once again, I was the low-life to Terry's jet setter. If we were doing a Variety Club lunch for TV I used to make a gag of the fact that he was inside, fronting the show, while I was given a minute or two outside the Hilton at the start of the programme. I would spin this yarn about not being allowed inside to mix with the stars and, because of my lowly position, having to stay outside in the wet, chained to the railings. I made a running joke of being allowed just so far and no more, like a kid pressing his nose up against the glass while the others got on with it. It became something of a trademark to say I was constantly on the fringes of this glamorous world, but always stopped at the door by the commissionaire when I actually tried to get in. If I was due to appear in the evening I would warn my morning audience to look closely for the potted palm in the foyer because that's where I would be, skulking in the shrubbery. I think that tapped a rich vein because there were many people who could associate with that feeling of being a bit of an outsider at these glamorous functions, people who enjoyed the glitter of the occasion but who knew they would never really be part of that showbiz world. They could recognise an ally in me, someone who was, quite literally, on the same wavelength as they were.

In those days I sometimes stood in for Terry – who seemed to get even more holidays from the radio than he does now from the TV! In fact at the time, playing the low-life card again, I used to say that if I asked for two weeks holiday the whole corporation used to go into nuclear meltdown but all Terry had to do was snap his fingers and he's away for a month!

Anyway, Terry's programme, which was always a delight to do, involved me in an incomprehensible rigmarole known as the Racing Bulletin. Terry called it 'Wogan's Winner'. I called it 'Moore's Horse' which was sometimes misconstrued as 'Moore's Whores'. It seemed to involve reciting a laundry list of broken nags who were threatening to bankrupt punters that afternoon. My lack of knowledge of the nagging world was so apparent that one day I was invited by the Clerk of the Course at Ascot to one of the meetings so that I might, at last, learn something. Not Royal Ascot, just Ascot – evidently there is a difference. 'Bring the old girl', I was told, 'Spot of lunch, a few gee-gees, a bit of tea, very informal'.

It was pouring with rain as Alma and I trudged for what seemed like miles from the station to the course and we arrived soaked to the skin. We dried ourselves off as best we could in the cloakroom and were shown to one of the luncheon rooms in the pavilion. The first person I saw there was the Queen Mum at the bar. I looked round at Alma, always ready with an encouraging word, 'Why in God's name didn't you tell me', she hissed, 'You said informal. I look as if I'm going to the shops. What do I say to her?'

'Just say, "Good morning, Ma'am"', I said as if I were any more at home than Alma was. Eventually we were introduced to the Royal Personage and I remember thinking, 'Please let her not look at my shoes'. These by now gave the impression – not exactly a false one – that I had walked through a ploughed field.

A group of about twenty of us now sat down to a light lunch, with the Queen Mother on the next table. Sitting next to me was the Dowager Duchess of Westminster, who appeared to own not only most of the famous racehorses in Britain, but most of the West End as well.

She was a formidable woman of powerful voice who smoked heroically. I took to her immediately. After the meal the coffee was accompanied by plates of sticky buns which were obviously one of the Duchess's weaknesses. She was constantly prodding me and saying in a husky stage whisper, 'Any more sticky buns, laddy?'

Alma and I chomped our way through this strange lunch party with increasing disbelief. Here we were at Ascot, two scallywags from the North of England, breaking bread with Royalty and leading members of the aristocracy, knowing that we had arrived there from Waterloo on a cheap day return.

By now Alma, 'Big Alma', was firmly established in Terry's show but when he left the breakfast programme to concentrate on TV work another name began to stick. Just as much as the old one it suggested that it was she who kept house, home, and husband together. And that much is *not* fiction.

It had its origins in our local off-licence which was run by a young couple, Tony and Stella. Stella worked in the shop, while Tony took on an advisory capacity at the back. I happened to ask Stella if we could hire glasses for a party and she replied with a nod in the direction of her husband sitting not twelve feet away, 'Oh, I think you'd better talk to Management about that'. Such a lovely, descriptive phrase. From then on Alma, the organiser, became 'Management' and used to feel quite flattered when perfect strangers would approach her and say, 'Hello, dear, are you Management?' Even now, months after the cancer announcement, letters and cards are still arriving at our home addressed simply to 'Ray Moore's Management, SE London'. And it always gives me a start when I hear the newsreaders on the radio say that 'Management has given in to union demands', or 'Mr Arthur Scargill will be meeting Management in the morning'. A strange assignation devoutly to be wished!

In the autumn of 1985 Dennis and I managed to inveigle the BBC into letting us loose on California for a second time. Our first attempts had clearly gone to our head and Deptford High Street was small scale for us now! This time our quarry was Stevie Wonder who was in town recording an album and who, so the message went, would be delighted to record an interview for us. The fact that we chose to descend on Los Angeles in the week of Jewish New Year was our first mistake. When we arrived it was like a ghost town. All the big agents, managers and artists had simply vanished, taking to the hills to celebrate the holiday. Stevie Wonder could not be reached and, even when we did make contact with his office, we were told that the

[175]

great star had now changed his mind about the interview and had, in fact, gone to New York. It seemed a long way to go to avoid us.

We then began to cast around for somebody else – anybody else to make the trip worthwhile. To return to London with nothing on tape after a week in the California sun would not have brought joy to the accounts department of Broadcasting House.

At this time Dennis and I had both entertained the hope that Sinatra, then coming up to his seventieth birthday, might deign to talk to us. We had already exhausted all the official channels to him and by devious means got the name of a man with whom Sinatra regularly played golf. For days we left messages with him, and then hung out at the Sportsman's Lodge for his call. None came. Like everybody else he had headed for the hills. In the event, seventieth birthday or not, Sinatra gave no interview to anyone so we were relieved to know that his refusal was not a personal vendetta against Dennis and me.

Our BBC skins were saved by two tremendous characters. One was Albert Hammond, writer of such classics as 'The Air that I Breathe', and 'It Never Rains in Southern California'. He gave us a wonderful interview and made an entertaining programme.

The other was a man I had admired for many years, Ray Conniff. It was his version of 'For All We Know' that I had used as a sign-off tune many times over the years on radio. He turned up at the hotel one afternoon and we decided to have a light lunch before getting down to business. Dennis and I ordered the 'all day breakfast', which meant, in effect, that there was so much on the plate that it took you all day to eat it. Conniff ordered the Seafood Salad, which turned up on a heaped platter the size of a bin lid. I had never seen so much seafood in a fishmonger's window before let alone as the main course. He gamely tucked into this, but retired, defeated, a quarter of the way through. After which none of us felt like working.

When we began the interview we realised it would be trickier than normal. Every time I asked a question, Ray Conniff would go rambling off in a totally unrelated direction, tossing out irrelevant observations and asking me eventually what the question was – by which time I had forgotten, too. It was the oddest, most disjointed conversation I have ever had and to edit the material into a programme we could broadcast was a feat of byzantine complexity. At least, though, we returned to London with something. The old firm of Moore and O'Keeffe had scraped by again.

Some months later Dennis and his assistant, Julie Pearce, Alma and I were on a train returning from a show when ideas were being discussed for future OB's and away days. We needed something different for the Children in Need Appeal that year but being on the air at 5.30 posed severe problems of credibility. There is not a lot of mileage in an outside broadcast in the pitch dark in the middle of the night. Alma had recently taken up jogging and she suggested some sort of fun-run.

Dennis and I roared helplessly and ordered more drinks. But slowly a lunatic scheme began to take shape. We would suggest to the BBC that in the week leading up to Children in Need day itself, we would do live outside broadcasts from five different sports stadiums around the country and invite joggers to come along and be sponsored for Children in Need. It was only on the next day that the whole barmy nature of this exercise became apparent – the middle of November, five thirty in the morning, pitch dark, probably pouring with rain, and we expected people to turn up and run round a track! It seemed like the greatest non-starter since the Ground Nut Scheme.

Whether the BBC thought that Dennis and I had finally gone certifiably insane and therefore, to prevent irrational violence, felt they should pander to our daft whims, I do not know. But, incredibly, they gave the green light to what became known as 'The Bog-Eyed Jogs'. The broadcasts were to come from Belfast, Glasgow, Manchester, and Birmingham leaving Dennis and Julie with the simple task of convincing stadium managers that we were serious about fun-runs at 5.30 in the morning in the middle of November.

Around this time I made the acquaintance of a glorious character by the name of Shag Connors, a West Country musician of extraordinary visage, with mutton chop whiskers and a bucolic, Mummerset accent. He released a record called 'The Cleanest Little Piggy in the Market' and, as a publicity stunt, borrowed a piglet from a local farm and brought it up to London on a lead. He then escorted the animal round various record shops and department stores in the West End. Fairly soon the Police were called and rapidly put an end to this piece of showmanship. Shag retired to the Northumberland Arms to lick his wounds and stood the piglet on the bar. Obviously the excitement proved too much because it promptly let fly with a bowel movement which ended up in Dennis's Guinness.

Shag, who lived in Bristol at the time, seemed to spend a lot of time in London and he would tell his wife Joyce that he had to go up to the West End to do some 'negotiating'. All this 'negotiating' took place on licensed premises and so at the end of a long hard day negotiating, he often had difficulty in remembering if any conclusions had been reached. As a result, he would have to return to London the following week to do a bit more negotiating. It was after one of these riotous forays up to the West End that Shag missed the last train back to Bristol and was forced to hitch a lift on the M4. After some hours a Porsche pulled up and offered him a ride all the way. They were cruising along the motorway at 90mph when Shag happened to remark what a fast car it was. 'This is nothing', the driver said, 'If I'm in the car on my own I do 120mph.'

'Good God', said Shag, 'Thank heavens I'm not with you when you're on your own.'

It was that sort of sense of humour which caused our professional lives to become intertwined for a short period. Shag was intrigued by a peculiar bit of nonsense that I had recited on radio for a long time, 'My father had a rabbit and he thought it was a duck, so he stuck it on the table with its legs cocked up . . .' One lunchtime, when I was present at a Shag Connors 'negotiating' session, he suggested he should write some more verses for this silly rhyme and then try and hoodwink some record company into letting us record it.

After some persuasion a little Irish record company agreed to release this musical masterpiece on the world. All we had to do first was record it. When Paul McCartney makes a new single he is often in the studio for months on end. When we did it we were in and out of a tiny BBC studio in Maida Vale by the time the pubs had opened. I very grandly said I would waive my fee and give the proceeds to Children in Need, confident that the only people who would pay real money for this tuneless travesty would be Mum, Alma, and Olive – the woman in the butcher's. My forecast was to turn out misguided and, the British public's capacity for masochism knowing no bounds, we were all in for a surprise.

The record was finally released at the end of October 1986 by which time all the planning for our outside broadcasts was complete, leaving us all in a state of mental uncertainty as to whether we were on the brink of some monumental, self-inflicted broadcasting disaster. In the regular and vivid nightmares, that were by now, a feature of my sleeping hours, I saw Dennis and me standing in darkness in the middle of a swamp, and totally alone. There was no way of turning back now.

On a wet Sunday afternoon before the first of the jogs we

checked into the Europa Hotel in Belfast, convinced the whole enterprise was destined to be an embarrassing shambles. We assembled in the bar at six o'clock. It was closed. The waiter told us the bar would not be open until seven o'clock but as we were residents, he asked us if we would like a drink while we were waiting. It seemed a perfect Irish compromise.

A gentle hurricane was blowing when we arrived at the Mary Peters track at 4.45am the following morning. To our utter amazement there were already twenty or so tracksuited bodies waiting for us. The stadium was in complete darkness except for the gleam of car headlights which barely illuminated the figure of one jogger scooting round the track in a wheelchair. He had evidently done twenty laps already. By the time the programme went on air there were a couple of hundred people present all tearing happily through the rain. Maybe this half-baked idea was going to work after all.

As the show went on more fellow lunatics turned up, many of them in costume. One old man appeared with his threadbare dog which became increasingly sodden in the incessant downpour as the man smoked an upturned pipe and plodded steadily round the track. In fact, one feature of the whole week was the number of sodden dogs we seemed to attract. By the time the programme came off air there were upwards of two thousand joggers all generating a palpable sense of fun and camaraderie. Not for the first time did I look at this crazy collection of folk and sense great waves of love from them. Love for me, the project and for our little team, Dennis, Julie and, of course, 'Management'. It had succeeded beyond anything we had dared hope.

Driving back to the hotel we watched as children set off for school, as women and men left for the shops and work and felt that here was an unremarkable scene which, in all its predictable normality, could have been acted out in Sheffield, or Croydon or anywhere in mainland Britain. Then we turned a corner and spotted a group of six teenage soldiers festooned in cruise missiles and Armalite rifles. After the friendship and the unity of the early morning jog the Troubles seemed more incomprehensible than ever.

The next stop was Glasgow. We were confronted with a spectacle which defied belief. A Caledonian monsoon had combined with a Siberian hurricane to produce a meteorological phenomenon which was guaranteed to intimidate all but the bravest. This was the day that the Controller of Radio 2, Bryant Marriott, had chosen to attend. Our first fundamental error was to choose a stadium that nobody had ever heard of and which even gnarled locals refused flatly to believe existed at all. It was, in fact, the Crown Point Stadium, just a short distance out of the city centre, a magnificently appointed place with full Olympic facilities. But nobody could find it.

When 5.30 came and I took the show on to the air Dennis and I were standing in the middle of the track surrounded by eight disconsolate joggers by now paddling round the course. Without resorting to telling downright lies on the radio I did have to cobble together a heavily embroidered report of the truth.

It was then that Bryant Marriott appeared on this pathetic scene. The rain had by now extinguished his pipe and he looked around at us all as if seriously doubting our sanity. The one consolation of that bleak morning was that Julie was keeping us constantly supplied with mugs of coffee liberally laced with malt whisky. This had the combined effect of keeping the blood circulating and giving Dennis and me a somewhat carefree attitude to the whole sorry business. As a result of such large quantities of coffee I was beginning to feel the urgent need of a lavatory, so in desperation I shot round to the back of the OB van to relieve myself on the rear offside wheel, which according to urban myth, is quite legal. While I was in full flood the record ended and I had to do the next link in rather peculiar circumstances. A radio show forces you to expose your personality to the world; exposure of *this* kind is not usually part of the contract. I was grateful to know we were not on TV.

It was dry and cold the following morning in Manchester and already a couple of hundred people were there when we arrived at the track at 5am. By the time we ended the show this number had swollen to several thousand. Among this raucous throng was the saxophonist extraordinaire, Johnny Roadhouse, who treated the crowd to a wobbly version of 'Happy Days are Here Again' as he padded heavily around the course. Stuart Hall, the great funny man Mike Craig and a wonderful Irish singer called Rose-Marie were with us too.

The next day, in Birmingham, was even better. We began to get the idea that these 'Bog-Eyed Jogs' were not such a daft idea after all. That morning coincided with the arrival of the Beaujolais Nouveau. A team of guys had driven overnight from France with one of the first consignments of this broad-shouldered brew and, hearing our broadcast on their car radio, had decided to make a detour and pop into the stadium. It would have been churlish not to sample this nectar so Dennis and I obliged. Swigging the stuff from the bottle at six-thirty in the morning presented a strange spectacle to the unwary.

There was another welcome arrival that day, in the form of Shag Connors who turned up in battered hat, smock and wellington boots looking like a superannuated Morris Man. He brought incredible tidings. Our record was actually selling and had, by then, reached the lower forties in the charts.

It was an odd experience to hear a disc jockey on Top of the Pops reading from a list of hit artists . . . Michael Jackson, Metal Mickey, Frankie Goes to Hollywood, Ray Moore, Men at Work . . . By Christmas the record had reached its peak and stuck at No24. I remember sneaking into a West End record store to see the sleeve of the record displayed prominently among all the other hits. I pulled my collar up and slunk away in case anyone recognised me as the perpetrator of this musical misdemeanour.

Early in the New Year of 1987 I was booked to host the International Ballroom Dancing Finals in Bournemouth. This TV assignment entailed broadcasting the morning radio show from Bournemouth, too, so Dennis and I were treated to the exciting prospect of a couple of days at the seaside in the middle of the worst January weather for years. There was no proper radio studio there but we managed to camp out in a well equipped broom cupboard at the back of the Bournemouth International Centre where the dance finals were being broadcast. There was barely room for Dennis and me but when an engineer turned up, none of us could turn round. There would have been more space in a telephone box.

The man of the Centre is a delightful man of Latin American extraction by the name of Jesus. I was rather taken by a little sign over the back door of the building which told us that Jesus was licensed not only for music and dancing but also for the retail of wines and spirits – holy spirits, presumably.

Our seaside interlude coincided with the worst blizzard ever to hit these parts and at one point, as the local paper reported, 'England was completely cut off from Bournemouth'.

Despite the weather, the cramped conditions and the hard work, it was great fun and, on a painfully slow skeleton rail service to Waterloo, Dennis and I congratulated ourselves on a good year, with the Children in Need project something of an ecstatic culmination. We toasted our future and that future looked bright. Little did I realise how wrong our prediction would turn out to be. By the time the summer came round, not five months away, the end of my career was in prospect and I would be facing the greatest trauma of my life.

[183]

[10]

The run-up to the unthinkable began innocently enough. For some weeks in the summer of 1987 I had become aware of a lump under my chin, small, at first, not quite the size of a pea but one which seemed daily to be increasing in size. It did not cause any pain, or interference. I felt as fit as an ox. Gradually I began to experience difficulty shaving around it and when Alma noticed it one day she became concerned. She nagged me mercilessly. 'If you don't ring Brian', she said, 'then I will'. Brian was our GP, a wonderfully mercurial Irishman with a faintly disdainful attitude to medicine.

We generally saw eye to eye. He was of the opinion that there are very few complaints which a doctor can actually cure and he believed that the majority of his patients needed the ministrations of a priest rather than him. I remember, for example, being on the air one morning with a dreadful cold and croaking my way through the broadcast with increasing difficulty. Not long after I got home, Brian turned up on the doorstep. 'I heard you on the radio this morning and you sounded bloody awful', he said, taking control of things immediately, 'I know it's no use giving you antibiotics because you'd only put them down the toilet. So go to bed, stay there for two days, drink this and shut up!' And he thrust a bottle of Irish whiskey into my hand.

Eventually I went to see him about the lump but, instead of being his bluff, hearty self, he became serious and gave me the number of a specialist he knew in Harley Street. By now the quiet unease I was feeling was escalating into a mood of blind fear and I let more weeks slip by, too terrified of what I might be told in Harley Street.

Eventually I went along to be ushered into one of those tall, cool rooms which seem to have changed little over the past sixty or seventy years. I told the man about my problem and he put on a pair of transparent gloves, fiddled inside my mouth and poked around my neck and throat. He, too, looked grave and I heard him muttering the word 'tumour'. He recommended a further opinion from a top ENT surgeon at a London hospital.

I held over the hospital visit for a while and instead scarpered along to the Northumberland Arms rather sharpish to get seriously involved in a planning meeting with Dennis. I arrived home in a tearful state brought on by a combination of drink and Harley Street. Alma, too, was frightened and upset by the news.

On September the 3rd 1987, the man at the hospital confirmed my blackest fear. It was a cancerous tumour in the floor of my mouth. There were, he said, two options open to me. The first was an immediate and massive blast of radiotherapy, coupled with a nauseous cocktail of drugs and extensive radical surgery. It appeared that this would involve hacking away at my tongue and jaw and cobbling together what was left of my face. All this would have left me with very little comprehensible speech. Pictures ran through my mind of The Man in the Iron Mask and The Phantom of the Opera. 'And the other option?' I asked him.

'Do nothing', he said. 'Either way the decision is philosophical'. He casually mentioned that we were talking of a life expectancy of about two years, whatever I did; although the surgery might – might – prolong that period. I emerged into the early autumn sunshine, lit a cigarette, and thought deeply.

What was I being offered? It seemed to me that the choice

was stark: life or existence. The doctors could offer me some possible extension to my existence but what I wanted was a quality of life. Rejecting the surgery (and, with it, the dubious promise it held out) meant coming to terms with the fact that the number of my days here on earth might be shortened but that the character of those remaining days would be enhanced. I pondered the implications of rejecting conventional treatment and wondered if I was up to it.

OK so the operation might just increase my life span by a few more months, maybe a year. But was I really interested in living to be one hundred just for the sake of it? Moreover, to consent to the mutilation of my face – to the destruction of my voice and speech – seemed an act of betrayal, a sell-out of all the ideals that had propelled me through life since I was a child. The end result, if I did nothing, might well be disfigurement and the collapse of speech, but to conspire in the process by voluntarily giving the go ahead to the knife with no guarantee of cure seemed morally wrong. 'I feel fine now', I remember thinking to myself, as I mentally made my decision. 'The work is going well. A lot of good things are coming up in the months ahead so why should I allow myself to be nailed down in an iron mask in some radioactive coffin? I shall carry on as long as I can and take one day at a time. Sod it, I'm going for broke!' Then I toddled off to do the commentary on an industrial film about the profound joys of marine paint.

Working on the BBC every day was the only kind of radio-therapy I needed and each delicious moment on air became more precious than ever. I greeted each new day as if it might be my last but told no-one about my condition. By this time dear old Gary Jackson's missives from the Cranley Crematorium contained a new kind of dark comedy; a woman wrote in one morning to inform me that I sounded as if I had one foot in the grave. I rather enjoyed the macabre unreality of it all. The music, too, took on a whole new significance and songs like 'For All We Know . . . we may never meet again' acquired a painful, new depth.

The word 'cancer' began to haunt me by night and by day. I was frightened. Alma and I discussed the decision I had reached and she agreed that if I had no confidence in the treatment offered then it could do no good. Brian, too, agreed that, on balance, I had done the right thing. None of this, however, dispelled the cloud of damp fear which wrapped itself around me.

We decided to tell as few people as possible; close family, of course, and Dennis and Julie, who over the years have been such dear friends. And, for legal reasons, I had to tell my boss on Radio 2. A new contract was about to be drawn up so they had to know in advance what my future prospects were likely to be. I could barely bring myself to ponder the unthinkable. After all this time, all this effort the BBC would one day have to replace me.

Two other emotions were grafted onto the fear and the sadness; emotions which, I was told, are common to many people suffering from cancer. Shame and guilt. I was plagued by the conviction that a sinful life had brought this dreadful judgement upon me. Had I not, after all, smoked too much, drunk too much, been too selfish, ignored Alma, worked too hard? God must clearly be in a towering rage with me if He goes to these lengths to teach me a lesson, I thought.

Throughout all the time that I was prey to this torment of self-recrimination I was, of course, hard at work. And I was grateful for my long years of training which had enabled me, once on air, to disguise my feelings and get on with the job in hand whatever my emotional state. A long time ago I had learnt that lesson and it was reinforced some months earlier by the experience of one poor guy who sadly had not.

[187]

I remember hearing a Radio 3 show hosted by a new presenter who managed to get himself worked up into a proper state. We all have bad mornings when things go wrong, but, in all circumstances, the presenter has to be cool. That is what we are paid for, after all. In this chap's case things got off to a bad start when he played in the wrong record. Then there were long gaps, scratches and records coming in half way through. So he opened the microphone and said, 'I'm sorry ladies and gentlemen, I seem to be having a slight problem here.' But then he added, by way of explanation something like, 'You see, I haven't been well these past weeks. The kids have been playing up and the whole thing's too much at the moment.'

So I kept my head (despite what was going on inside it) and got down to work. I was still doing trailers between programmes on BBC1 sitting there at the microphone, out of vision, bawling, 'Entertainment tonight on BBC1' and then following it with a run-down of half a dozen of the most tedious shows imaginable. Outside the BBC life was also hectic. Many firms these days make videos, not only for launching new products, but also for training staff and, although they never go out on air, they do get a showing at Trade Conferences and Fairs like the Ideal Home Exhibition or the Motor Show. They all need the services of a narrator. I did so many that I often forgot what I had done. On one occasion, as I was wandering around an industrial exhibition at the G-Mex Centre in Manchester I heard my voice extolling the virtues of clay tiles, roofing felt and a disinfectant for cleaning pub lavatories. For some obscure reason I also became the flavour of the month with the double glazing fraternity.

We recorded these commentaries at odd little studios around London's Soho and quite often I would turn up to a session not knowing what on earth I would be flogging. As I was labouring through an uplifting piece for the Concrete and Mortar Association once, I heard from the studio behind me Gloria Hunniford singing the praises of gas cookers. In the more penny-pinching studios even the luxury of a separate booth for the narrator did not exist. Instead he would stand in the middle of a room at a sort of lectern and read the commentary to the tribes of clients, agents, and production people sitting in rows three feet from his face. Inevitably, as the recording proceeded, at least one member of this strange audience would develop a coughing fit or drop an ashtray, and the recording would start again. Coughs, sniffs and sneezes alternated with the whoopee-cushion effect of buttock on leather as bored executives sought discreetly to shift their weight from cheek to cheek. Again the recording would restart and it became something of a competition to see how far the narrator could get before he was back to the beginning again. A script that might have taken twenty minutes to record in a booth regularly took an hour in this open studio after constant interruption from the extraneous noise of bodily functions.

Voice overs for television commercials also had their own ridiculous rigmarole. The vision element was contained on a loop of film which endlessly repeated itself. I, meanwhile, would chunter through the script over and over again, making it fit the pictures. After five or six minutes of this, often with no direction, the 'director' would say, 'Right. Let's put one down'.

Inevitably he would judge the reading to lack the right artistic intonation appropriate to the product in question so we would go on to 'Take 2'. We once got to 'Take 27', by which time I was becoming thoroughly peeved at whoever's soap powder I was supposed to be so enthusiastic about. As the booking drew to a close the director said, 'Let's just listen to "Take 3" again'. This, they discovered, was as near to what they wanted as they were likely to get. Knowing a fair bit about reading a script by now I often wondered quite why they needed to have bothered with twenty-four extra takes in the first place.

Many a time a director would say, 'Yes, Ray, fine. Very nice reading. But could we try it again with a touch more Patrick Allen in it?'

'If they wanted Patrick Allen', I muttered to myself through clenched teeth, 'why the devil didn't they book him at the start?'

By the autumn of 1987 the BBC had finally decided, in the face of reason and common sense, that they would like our little team to be entrusted with another week of 'Bog-Eyed Jogs' for the current year's Children in Need Appeal. Dennis, Julie and I began to get down to the serious business of deciding on the venues, which often involved more riotous planning meetings at the Northumberland Arms where often little more would be decided other than whose turn it was to buy the drinks. The Jogs had clearly caught the imagination of someone rather high up in the BBC hierarchy because we were officially offered the services of a press and publicity person, a baleful fellow of lugubrious demeanour called Graham Lambourne, whose role it was to tour the various locations to give advance warning of our party of Radio 2 lunatics organising the charity appeal. We wanted, at all cost, to avoid a rerun of the previous year's Glasgow fiasco. Graham would also be responsible for organising the sponsorship forms and publicity material and be on hand to gee-up the local press, radio and television.

One Friday, in the middle of one of our more exuberant planning meetings Dennis came up with a suggestion for another musical anthem to accompany this year's enterprise. He produced some lines written by our own West Country Lyricist and musical adviser, Shag Connors, who had produced a song entitled, naturally enough, 'The Bog-Eyed Jog'. With our last musical triumph still ringing in our ears, we decided there and then, that it would be a tragedy to spare the British public another chance to hear us in full voice.

We all found it rather strange that Shag himself failed to turn up at the recording session. His son, Martin, however, took his place and explained to us all that his old Dad was not too well. In fact Shag was, at the time, desperately ill with lung cancer, and he died the day after our recording. Genuine sadness hung over the team at the passing of this wonderfully eccentric and kind man. We all set off for the West country for the funeral and when we arrived the priest asked me if I would say a few words as a sort of eulogy to Shag. I agreed, of course, but it was an enormously difficult thing to do. Here I was mourning his death, having been told that my own final exit was not very far away. I cried that day not only for Shag but also for myself.

By now Alma and I were beginning to get into a blind panic about the future. Questions raced unanswered though my mind. What are we going to do for money? Will we have to sell the house? Will Alma cope? Would I be going to a hospice? Feeling that I was about to hit the soup at any minute, we made our wills and put everything in our joint names.

By now the tumour was getting larger and – the thing I feared most – my speech was beginning to be affected. I also noticed that my bottom teeth were starting to wobble loose and I could feel them flapping about in the breeze as I was doing those hard-sell TV trailers for Sportsnight and Grandstand. I half expected two or three to come loose on air and flutter into sight for the opening credits. I had also, by this time, grown a beard to disguise the lump so that I not only sounded odd but looked peculiar, too. I consulted my dentist who sent me off in turn to a specialist who once again offered me the ferocious power of radiotherapy, drugs, and radical surgery. This combination still did not attract me, not least because I thought it pointless, when I felt perfectly well, to be making myself feel ill on purpose. I vowed to make each moment of each day a bonus.

The dentist did not seem to understand and, like many other doctors I had seen, grew faintly angry, taking my refusal to accept treatment as some sort of implied criticism of his profession. And I suppose, in a very limited way, it was. I did defer to their scientific knowledge but I felt that healing should be more of an art than a science. Alma and I studied the whole area of healing and homeopathy and concluded they could not all be cranks and lunatics. There must be something in the notion of taking the body as a whole (mind and spirit included) rather than seeing it automatically as separate bits that can be hacked off if they cause trouble. Some of the doctors we met were very supportive but others were very sniffy about the whole thing. I sympathised most with those who felt my course of cure was complementary to theirs and who did not accuse me of seeking a complete replacement to what they had to offer. All too often the high-tech approach offered, in effect, a killing process. It was set up to kill the cancer and I felt very strongly that cure could be approached from another direction, namely that by mobilising the body's natural healing powers something positive would emerge. Many people have disagreed with me but I felt instinctively that this was the right course for me.

I remember being seen by two doctors at one point; an older man and a younger man. The younger chap had been trying for months to get me to have the full Chernobyl blast while the older man, more sympathetic to my own worries, was at least prepared to consider my philosophical outlook. During one session the older man drew me aside and said with a smile, 'I should say that my junior colleague thinks I'm being too soft on you'. Surely it was no part of the doctor's job to make things *hard* for me. It's my body, for God's sake. We reached a compromise. I would consent to light radiation treatment but the radical surgery I refused.

Having brought to my dentist's attention the wobbly teeth I was by now aware that my speech was being affected at an unpredictable rate. I began seriously to wonder if it would hold out until the 'Bog-Eyed Jogs', at the end of November. The memory of the previous year was still so sweet that I was desperately keen to repeat it. The uncertainty of it, however, brought me face to face once again with the fact that the days on my beloved radio were numbered. And great waves of depression would wash over me. It was too awful to contemplate so I did my best to banish such thoughts from my mind. When the alarm clock rang at 3.30 I thanked God I had another day on the air.

The cancer was first diagnosed at the end of July and by the end of January my career was at an end. The six months of early alarm calls and morning trips down the Old Kent Road burned with an emotional intensity I had never experienced. Externally the sights were the same; the punk girl with the stove pipe hair, the late night drunks and the Ferret Cleaning Company, but my appreciation of them all had mellowed. I became immensely aware of life's fragility, immensely tolerant of its imperfections. Each second just alive and breathing took on an added value. But some mornings I was crippled with despair, knowing that the game had a finite limit and I was now approaching it. Then it became so hard to call up the energy to go on with the morning show, to be witty and to disguise the fact that I was steadily going downhill. At times like that a weariness I had never known before invaded my whole being. I knew what tiredness was – having got up at 3 o'clock in the morning for so long, how could I not know – but as the battle with the cancer was joined there was a sort of weariness to the bone which went beyond all tiredness, as though sitting up and breathing required every ounce of effort I possessed. Making it to the studio offered some respite. There the sweetness of every moment was more intense than ever.

By now the location for the jogs had been settled. We could start on Monday in Gateshead, then on to the Meadowbank

Stadium in Edinburgh on Tuesday, the Mary Peters track in Belfast on Wednesday, Cwmbran in South Wales on Thursday and, to finish, the Mountbatten Centre in Portsmouth on the Friday. This time every single venue had the whiff of success about it. Which is more than could have been said for my record of Shag's song, 'The Bog-Eyed Jog'. It was greeted by the public with a mixture of derision and apathy as it clawed its way sluggishly to the low sixties in the charts before finally giving up the ghost and fizzling out entirely. Still, I consoled myself with the thought that even Paul McCartney does not always make it to number 1.

We all met up in the bar of King's Cross Station at lunchtime on Sunday. Our little team of Dennis, Julie, Alma and our publicity man, Graham, was now joined by our engineer, Johnny White, a man of somewhat ruddy complexion who, after a couple of drinks would go a sort of vivid puce. To say he was vivid puce for most of the week is something of an exaggeration.

The following morning the Gateshead Stadium looked more like the set for a modern day staging of The Retreat from Moscow. But even the gale and the blizzard did not deter hundreds and hundreds of people from turning out at 5.30am to raise thousands of pounds for the appeal. Two glorious lunatics by the name of Brian and Dave from a woollen factory in Bradford joined this ragged army and presented the team with outsize woollen sweaters bearing the Children in Need logo. I lived in mine all week – indeed it was so large I sub-let part of it to spectators who turned up unprepared for the weather.

Brian and Dave were determined to follow us to all five venues and equally determined to make a bizarre contribution to the cause. In addition to jogging for charity they brought along an enormous iron bedstead on which rested a tailor's dummy. At the bed head stood five pub optics containing vodka, whisky, brandy, gin and rum. They proposed pushing this odd contraption as they jogged round the course. The device proved quite useful in the end because each time they passed the place from where I was delivering the commentary, I would casually lean over and fortify my coffee cup with a generous slug of brandy – purely to keep out the cold, of course, as my father used to say.

As the week wore on the two of them became disenchanted with carting the bedstead around so they unhitched the optics and spent their time at each stadium helping themselves to generous measures. They found it a congenial way of passing a couple of hours and, as I recall, found little spare time for much jogging.

At every venue we attracted a whole menagerie of runners in all manner of animal disguises. They came as ostriches, rabbits, ducks, pantomime horses and odd shaped, unidentifiable furry mutants. Surveying this lot I felt like the ringmaster of some nightmare circus. There was even a musical interlude, too, when, in Cwmbran Stadium, a sixty strong Welsh choir sang forceful laments from their varied repertoire, from Cym Rhondda to 'The Bog-Eyed Jog'.

I overstepped the mark flying out from Belfast, I remember. The cabin crew suggested I ask the passengers for a contribution to Children in Need but did not expect me to go out on the tannoy saying, 'This is an unofficial hijack and nobody leaves the aircraft until everyone has given to Children in Need!' Realising they were en route from Northern Ireland a lot of the passengers looked seriously apprehensive and perturbed by this merry jape. In spite of that we got them to part with £57.

After Cwmbran we were due to travel on to Portsmouth by train from Newport. Dennis and I discovered our train had no bar so we felt it necessary to build up reserve stocks to fortify us for the journey. Off we went to Newport in search of an off-licence. For nearly half an hour we traipsed around without success, reaching the conclusion that the worthy folk of Newport were either teetotal or had decided on a policy of Prohibition. In desperation we stopped a man and asked for directions to the nearest off licence. Thinking we were a pair of alcoholics on the run he said, 'What are you worried about? If you hang about for five minutes the pubs will be open'.

The Mountbatten Centre in Portsmouth was our last venue and probably the most successful. Many hundreds were there well before dawn but their numbers swelled into thousands as the morning wore on. Among them was Rolf Harris, who turned up dressed in a strange looking poncho affair that could just possibly have been one of his mother's old tablecloths. Also there was a wonderful bunch of kids from the Littlemead School in Chichester with their headmaster, Mr Bowler. They threw themselves into the event with great enthusiasm and raised thousands for Children in Need. I did not realise it then, but before very long I was to pay another poignant visit to the Littlemead School.

The whole week had been such a happy and entertaining success that on the train back we held an impromptu party to celebrate. We climbed aboard as on a brewery works outing and proceeded to lay heavily into the assorted bottles of Algerian bellywash we had accumulated. On arrival at Waterloo, tired, ragged and not a little dishevelled, we must have looked like the remnants of a small defeated army.

As the weeks drew on towards Christmas '87, the tumour under my chin was not only getting bigger but also developing some exceptional little habits of its own. It had, by this time, broken through the skin and had a tendency to weep a noxious oily liquid from time to time. To do the radio broadcasts in the morning I had to go armed with a box of tissues to dab the thing periodically. One of the engineers wondered why it was that my beard was leaking. Socially, too, things were becoming increasingly awkward. It is not very pleasant to be sitting next to a chap at a dinner party and to see him constantly mopping his chin with Kleenex. For the New Year's Eve broadcast I finally had to admit defeat and wear a dressing on the tumour. Inevitably, everyone advised me to keep my chin up while I, by way of explaining my facial peculiarity, would mutter fairytales about a bad abscess.

I was also aware that the clarity of my speech was fading quite alarmingly. I began to pray to God that I would be guided into knowing when I was no longer good enough on air. The worst thing I could imagine was that I would press on past the point beyond which I was no longer professionally acceptable. If I could not give my best I did not want to carry on. I had been given a good voice and, with God's help, cared for and nurtured it. If it sounded slurred and sloppy then it would be upsetting for everybody and I owed it both to the listeners and to myself to give the best I could.

In addition my mouth was becoming increasingly painful, like a deep nagging toothache which kept me awake at nights, making the mornings harder than ever. Then there was the tiredness which was more than tiredness; that mental, physical and spiritual exhaustion which felt as if I had reached my sell-by date. Things were clearly approaching a climax. Of that much I had advance warning when one night the tumour began to bleed. I dashed blindly to the bathroom and leaned over the sink while the blood gushed out like a running tap. It lasted for some hours after which I went to bed swathed in towels in case it decided to perform a second midnight matinée. I slept fitfully, fearing the worst. What if it should start bleeding in the studio, in a restaurant, on the Underground? These bleeding sessions (to be taken both as description and execration) became increasingly frequent but, mercifully, always at home and usually at night. Then one day I was confronted with the unthinkable.

I had had a most convivial lunch with my brother, Don, in an Italian restaurant in Charlotte Street, a fashionable spot squeezed between the Post Office Tower and Soho. When we came out it was pouring with rain so I hailed a cab, said goodbye to Don, and made my way to Charing Cross station heading for home. As we approached Trafalgar Square I looked down at my coat and it was spattered with large red stains. My shoes were the same. I stopped the cab and got out in the teeming rain. The blood was now flowing in torrents down my shirt, coat and trousers as I tried pathetically to stem the flow with the few tissues I had in my pocket. To the passers-by it must have looked like a bungled attempt to behead myself. It was clear that I could not sit on the train in this appalling state so I made a bee line into the Gents at the Charing Cross Hotel, where the blood poured into the sink and onto the white floor tiles. It soon began to look like the scene of eight horrific murders so I dashed to a cubicle, locked myself in, and hoped it would eventually stop its antics. Three quarters of an hour later it was still streaming. Then there was a furious banging on the cubicle door. It was the hotel security man demanding to know what was going on. Obviously someone had spotted the blood-spattered sink and concluded that a small massacre was going on in the Gents. I reluctantly opened the door and stood there tearful, explaining to the man what the problem was. He was visibly shaken, not only by my gory state but by the fearful, bloody scene inside the cubicle. He called an ambulance and rang Alma with the details.

The hospital casualty department could not stop the flood either but they bandaged me up sufficiently to get home. They strapped what appeared to be half a dozen towels under my chin and then tied the dressing up on the top of my head with a bow. I emerged from casualty looking like the Queen of Sheba.

It was shortly after this episode that I got a letter from Mr

Bowler at the Littlemead School in Sussex to say that he and the parents were so proud of the children's efforts for Children in Need, that he was throwing a small celebration lunch party at the school to honour their achievement. Would I care to be present to accept the cheque for the charity? This was fixed for the end of January and I said that I hoped very much to be there. I had serious reservations, however, because I knew full well the local press world would be there and if the tumour suddenly started its Niagara impressions again, it could lead to all sorts of great embarrassments. Dennis, who by now knew the full story, agreed to embark on another away day with me.

As January ticked by I sensed my speech was becoming less and less acceptable on the radio. Every live broadcast is recorded as it is going out on air and, in the past, I used to review these recordings periodically to check if certain stories or gags had worked. Now I was too frightened of these tapes, fearful of what I might hear. I was horrified at the thought of ever having to put the BBC in the awful position of having to say to me, 'Look, son, you're not up to it! Thank you very much. Good night'. That was a job I had to do for myself.

Sunday January the 24th 1988 was the day of the Laurence Olivier Awards, to be broadcast live on television with me booked to do the voice-over commentary. As the award-winning actors and directors were named on stage I would be muttering away in the undergrowth about their previous amazing achievements – all to be slotted in the space it took them to walk from their seats to collect the trophies. It was a role I had cheerfully played a thousand times and I knew precisely what was expected of me. I was familiar with that lovely, exciting, egocentric feeling of hearing the audience go quiet as my voice boomed out across the auditorium, 'Ladies and Gentlemen, BBC1 is proud to present The Laurence Olivier Awards for 1988'. But this time I was scared.

[199]

I had asked Alma to watch the transmission carefully and then to tell me honestly if she could detect any peculiarities in my speech. I turned up at the Victoria Palace at midday for the rehearsals wearing a somewhat lumpy dressing which Alma had applied, and carrying the address of the nearest hospital in case of emergency. The director of the show wondered whether somebody had tried to shut me up by cutting my throat. I was relieved to think that my contribution to the broadcast had gone reasonably well, and doubly relieved, as I sat in my commentary position backstage, that my chin had at least had the decency to behave itself in front of Elaine Page and Stephen Sondheim. Prince Edward, of course, was also there that night – the man I had kept waiting in the wings – and the director had arranged for him to meet those who had worked on the show. I explained that I had to be up early for the show next day and that I ought to leave. I just felt that to have a haemorrhage on the stage of the Victoria Palace in front of Prince Edward and three thousand people would not have added greatly to the hilarity of nations.

I arrived home to find Alma depressed and in tears. She said nothing at first but shook her head gravely. It was obvious what her verdict on my performance was, and if my speech was that bad on television, then it was certain that radio would exaggerate these lapses of clarity. I was so concerned that people would think I was drunk or drugged that I vowed to listen back to one of the recordings of the radio show that week. The most convenient morning to do it was the following Thursday, the day when Dennis and I were due to be travelling down to Chichester for the Littlemead School presentation. Having had one or two more bleeding sessions that week, and very little sleep, I weaved and tottered my way through the Thursday morning broadcast. Initially I felt very bad, then the old 'radio-therapy' worked its magic again, and towards the end I was feeling happy and confident and, like old times, wallowing in the fact of being live on the air. During the course of the programme I did a birthday dedication for an old lady called Alice Arrowsmith, whose name gave me a moment or two of hesitation. I managed to pronounce it all right – or so I thought – and sailed on. At eight o'clock I settled down with coffee and a cigarette to listen back to the recording. The truth, slow to dawn but inescapable, hit me with a sickening clarity. I was no longer good enough. When the dedication came up I sounded as if I were talking about someone called 'Alish Allowsmish'. I remember a black feeling in the depth of my soul as I said to myself out loud, 'That's it, son, the game's up.'

Later that morning Dennis and I caught the train to Chichester from where I asked him to ring the Head of Radio 2 with the news that, after the weekend I could no longer continue on air. After the hilarity of all our other away days this was a painful excursion for us both. We arrived at the Littlemead reception with me carrying a holdall containing half a dozen towels in case of sudden incident. Then as we chatted to the people there I kept popping to the loo to check that no ominous red patches had appeared anywhere. One of the guests there that day was the astronomer Patrick Moore who was also, for some reason, sporting a medical bandage on the side of his face. He looked sagely at my padded chin and said, 'I'll tell you about mine if you tell me about yours'. We looked like the bandage section of a Red Cross open day exhibition.

During lunch Dennis rang the Head of Radio 2, Frances Line, and told her of my decision. She asked him to see her as soon as he returned to London. I got home by late afternoon and was hardly through the door when the phone rang. It was Frances who said that I was obviously in some state of distress and therefore I should not try to get in to do the programme the following morning. I explained that this thing was not going to get worse so I would certainly be willing and able to do the show. I pleaded with her to let me savour the consummate joy of one last broadcast but this she gently and quite rightly refused. The BBC would issue a press statement in the morning. And that was it. It was over. Not with a bang but a whimper. Suddenly the full, terrible finality hit me and I started sobbing uncontrollably.

The end might have been easier to bear if I could have viewed it as some sort of early retirement. But that was never going to be possible. Radio meant far more than just a job to me; it was my life. I used to have long battles with my accountant about pensions and annuities and nest eggs for when I gave up work but I told him, 'I don't intend to "give up work", I'll carry on doing this until I drop'. Retirement was unimaginable, a life without broadcasting was unimaginable. If I had not had this sense of vocation it might have been easier to rationalise. But for God to turn round to me and say 'That's it. You've done enough, Ray. I can use no more of what you've got to offer', was a lot to take in. When the whole motivation of your life is in an instant gone, what do you do? I did the only thing I could. I looked into a void and cried for a week.

During this time I was helped by lots of people, by friends I knew well and by perfect strangers whom I had never seen before. Reading all the nice things that were written in the papers made it worse for a time, as if underlining the total injustice of it all. It was like being a witness at my own funeral. But then more letters came, and more, and it was clear that I was being supported out there somewhere by a powerful current of love. Many of the really big names from this business wrote out of genuine concern and sorrow, often with offers of practical help if I needed it. And then there were the ordinary people who hardly knew what to say but who felt the need to write. They assured me of their prayers, told me there were Masses being said for me and even offered their phone numbers and addresses 'just in case'. Since I have come off air people have written as never before, telling me that while I was on I was a great help to them, so, now that the roles were reversed, they wanted me to be assured of their help in return. There were those who wrote in to thank me for giving them a smile in the morning, for lifting them from deep depression to face the day or simply for making them realise that they were not alone in the world at 5.30 in the morning.

The letters were all the more precious because I had not had the time to say goodbye. On Thursday I had done the show and on Friday, with no announcement, I was off for good. And yet for all that, there were people out there who, for reasons which defy logical explanation, knew there was something wrong. A letter from one lady proved it.

About three months before doing the final broadcast I was doing some work in Sussex – in Chichester again, as it turned out – and, with a few hours to spare before setting off for home, I decided to pop into the cathedral for choral evensong. When I arrived I was far too early and spent another hour alone in this vast, impressive place. As I was sitting there reflecting on the disease, I was suddenly interrupted by the sound of a vacuum cleaner, and a person noisily hoovering the carpet. I was mildly irritated by this, and mentioned it the following day on the programme. I thought nothing more of it until a letter arrived from a lady who had sensed something very strange from that minor event. She started off by expressing her sadness that I would no longer be doing the programme but went on to say, 'But do you remember that time in Chichester when you were disturbed by the noise? I knew there was something seriously wrong then. If you had been any old tourist you wouldn't have been upset by that sort of thing. You were clearly there to commune with your Maker. I could tell that'. I was amazed. I had forgotten the Chichester story completely but the listeners hadn't. They knew more about me than I did about myself sometimes. They could read the signs.

Among the offers of help were many from people who suggested I consult a healer. And I have been helped beyond measure by some very impressive healers of great power. One was Phil Edwardes who brought me great tranquillity. But Michael Aspel had had a lot of help from a healer in Sussex called Betty Shine when his son was ill in Australia and he recommended this particular person. So, too, did Michael Bentine who had spoken to her much earlier about his daughter. I telephoned Betty out of the blue one Sunday when a story about me had appeared in the Sunday Express. She happened to be reading the paper at the time and was, apparently, wondering when I was going to call – even though she had no idea who I was nor had ever met me.

I travelled down to see her and got some comfort from discussing things with her. She took the line that many cancer sufferers are the nicest possible people and that their niceness can sometimes be their undoing! They are unwilling to show anger or annoyance and simply bottle it up with the result that these forces are repressed deep inside them and come out in all sorts of negative ways. The cancer, in part, she said could be attributable to my not feeling at ease either with myself or other people. For too long I had had a low opinion of myself and this 'dis-ease' was now the result.

I visited her once and she recorded our conversation on a cassette recorder, both before and during a healing session, and then played back the result. The conversation at the beginning was normal and clear but as we moved into the healing section it grew more and more distorted until what sounded like electrical interference made the dialogue inaudible. 'It's not a trick', Betty said, 'it's just to show the powerful forces that we have harnessed in this healing process'. On the way back home I felt pain in my jaw such as I had never felt before – like toothpicks being driven into my jaws. It lasted about an hour and then, shortly after I had arrived back, the healer phoned and asked how bad the pain had been. I asked her how she could possibly know that I had been experiencing such pain and she replied simply that 'she knew'. She knew, she said, that we had released those forces during the session and that, knowing there was a monumental battle going on within my system, she was not surprised that the pain had been so acute. She told me not to view that pain as an entirely negative thing; that, too, could be part of the healing process. I have to admit it did not make me feel a whole lot better.

Consulting healers like this is a bit of a change for me and yet side by side with my down-to-earth nature is an intuitive mystic part which is not quick to dismiss these things.

But certainly these people have great strength of mind and, by their example, they have encouraged me to find that strength, too. One technique I tried to use was that of visualising the cancer as something totally alien to my body which my body could fight off. You do hear stories of a cancer having a finite life which your healthy body can outlive. I do not know how true the stories are but certainly it was a process which made sense to me – that of mobilising my inner resources to re-establish health in a diseased part. But, most of all, by actively taking a hand in my own healing – rather than passively submitting to surgery – I was doing something positive. I was taking the responsibility for myself upon myself. And merely by doing that I gained some comfort.

And then, when all else seemed to fail, I was driven to the only remaining solutions. Submission and endurance.

Fighting the cancer but submitting to God were two strong lessons taught me recently by Harry Read, the Salvation Army man who has been on hand when I needed him most. He was one of the first people I told of the cancer. By now, of course, he had been promoted higher in the Army and was a very busy man but he dropped everything that day to be with me when I needed his reassuring words. With great understanding he listened to my anger, pain and bewilderment and enabled me, almost by his presence alone, to bear the intolerable. He also taught me how to pray. He told me to cup my hands, to imagine them holding all my burdens and my sorrows, and to hand them over physically to God for Him to take. Shortly after he wrote a special prayer for me:

> Lord.
> You know my heart, and how I shrink
> From threat of any further pain.
> How this affects me as I think
> And turmoil starts in me again.
>
> Why cancer, Lord? I'm mystified.
> Why should it strike, and why strike me?
> Why take my cells within its stride
> As though by some divine decree?
>
> But calmer thoughts speak of Your love;
> Remind me that You always care;
> That in the hardest times we prove
> That where we are – the Christ is there.

Though suffering is mystery
Beyond our power to understand,
You are life's true reality,
And courage comes from Your sweet hand.

In all this, of course, I have failed to mention the greatest human source of strength I have: Alma. She and I have clung together so closely over the past months that together we have experienced more highs and lows than we ever thought we could in a lifetime. Her strength has kept me afloat when I felt close to going under. Sometimes in the really dark nights of the soul, when there seems no conceivable way out I recall Scott Fitzgerald's phrase, 'the fear of death can become a longing for death'. But Alma has been there to draw me back.

And she too is, privately, just as fearful as I. Sometimes I came home to see that she had been crying, despite the great strength she has presented to the world. At moments like that, when the world seemed so black that we would question the whole point of it, we came together more intensely than before. Cancer is such a sordid business; not like fading away with the vapours on clean white sheets. This is such an untidy, smelly, horrible thing.

In spite of all, the past months have become sweeter than ever. Waking each morning is a precious bonus, walking round the heath, seeing friends; all this has acquired a new depth. And if the days turn out to be shorter then, together, we will have known that they have been all the richer.

As a child in Cherry Close I always hated going to bed. Dad would say 'There's always another day tomorrow', and I would be unmoved. I would be listening to the wireless and Mum would say the same thing, 'Switch it off, Ray, there's another day tomorrow'. But I used to fight against that and think, 'I don't care about tomorrow, now is what I'm enjoying and I want to hang on to it'. It is a childhood memory that has haunted me over the past months because now, for very different reasons, I dare not even think about tomorrow.

And so I carry on, one day at a time, enjoying each precious moment as it comes along. There is a line in a Tennessee Williams play in which he talks about someone plagued by bouts of depression. The image he uses to describe it is that of having a 'blue devil' perched on your shoulder constantly taunting you with sadness and sorrow. The only way out, he says, is to endure it because if you do, sooner or later the blue devil will tire and go away. It may come back but all you have to do is quietly endure it an hour at a time, a minute at a time.

So that is what we do. We endure it a day at a time and are grateful for the happiness and the love that Alma and I can share. It can be hard at times but I say to myself, 'I can still see beauty around me, I can still hear music. I still have Alma'. If this is endurance then at least it has its compensations.

And so I stare that blue devil in the face and he knows I have got him worried. He may get me in the end but I am determined to give him a damn good run for his money.